MAUI

MAUI

A HISTORY

*Originally Mowee: A History
of Maui the Magic Isle*

BY CUMMINS E. SPEAKMAN, JR.
UPDATE BY JILL ENGLEDOW

Mutual Publishing

Publishing Log of *Maui: A History*

1978   Original hardcover, first edition by The Peabody Museum under the title *Mowee: An Informal History of the Hawaiian Island*

1981/1984 Softcover printings by Pueo Press

2001   Updated edition by Mutual Publishing under the title *Mowee: A History of Maui the Magic Isle*

2014   Updated further for the period 2000-2013 with title change to *Maui: A History*

Note: Original Hawaiian spellings have not been changed from the original edition to remain representative of the time in which the book was first written.
The original introduction by Cummins E. Speakman, Jr. is now the Preface.

Library of Congress Catalog Card
Number: 2001118590

ISBN: 978-1939487-39-1

Second Printing, September 2014
Third Printing, October 2015
Fourth Printing, March 2017

Mutual Publishing, LLC
1215 Center Street, Suite 210
Honolulu, Hawai'i 96816
Ph: (808) 732-1709
Fax: (808) 734-4094
email: info@mutualpublishing.com
www.mutualpublishing.com

Printed in South Korea

To Julie, Jay and Chris,
and
the people of Maui
for whom
this book has been written

TABLE OF CONTENTS

PREFACE*

The island of Maui is the second largest in the Hawaiian chain. In some respects, it is also the richest, and, due to its geographical position between the islands of Hawai'i and Oahu, it has played a rather special role in Hawaiian history.

Yet Maui's own history has been neglected. So far as I know, it has not been treated separately but only in fragments in general histories of the Islands. I became aware of this as I found opportunities to study Pacific and Hawaiian history and while offering a course during the winter of 1976-1977 in the History of Maui for Chaminade University of Honolulu.

Various field trips with County Parks personnel and my students took us to archaeological sites on the island. Information from these, together with data gained on hikes and horseback trips during a decade-long residence on Maui, were welcome supplements to the readings we were doing for the course.

Confirming the need for a history of the Valley Isle from scholars, librarians, visitors, county personnel, teachers, and students, I decided to try my hand at writing a history of "my own special island." During the Bicentennial year of 1976, it occurred to me that the publication of the island's history would be an appropriate project for 1978, the bicentennial of Captain James Cook's first sighting of Maui on November 26, 1778.

The work went slowly until the summer of 1977 when I found interesting material on Maui's history in the libraries of the British Museum and especially in the Public Record Office in London. By that time I had decided that the book would be about Maui, the island, rather than the county which includes Moloka'i, Lana'i, and Kaho'olawe.

In September 1977, the Peabody Museum of Salem, Massachusetts, was approached and the project presented to Dr. Ernest S. Dodge, the Director, himself the author of seven books, four of them on Pacific history. The Museum was interested. The project fitted well with its series of publications on Pacific history,

---

and the book was seen as a suitable recognition of the bicentennial year of Captain Cook's voyages to the Hawaiian Islands, which are represented in the Museum by an important ethnographic collection.

Financial support followed from the Eaton Foundation, Inc. and the Willard C. Tilson Foundation. Ernest Dodge acted as senior editor, and as copy editor, Philip C. F. Smith's contribution can be seen in the excellence of the book's design as well as the careful editing of every section in it. It was a privilege to work with these distinguished scholars and I acknowledge with deep thanks their help and the support of the foundations. With publication assured, work on the book resumed in earnest in October 1977.

In writing this informal history, I have tried to tread the fine line between a scholarly work and one that is written for the general reader. The sources and references are all found in the sections following the main text, where they are easily referred to by scholars, and footnotes are generally provided within the text. Emphasis on the subtitle is on "informal" as this does not pretend to be a comprehensive history. No doubt other historians will take exception to some interpretations, although I have been careful to qualify statements, especially about events before 1820, by saying "it is believed" or "it is said that."

Many people in Hawai'i helped with this book: more than I can acknowledge by name. Most of all, I am indebted to Inez Ashdown, unofficial County Historian for kokua from her research, for teaching me appreciation for the old Hawaiian culture, and for encouragement and inspiration. Genie Bakris at the Kahului Library never hesitated to take on my most difficult (and often obscure) requests for information and acted as "general reader" for the first chapters. Captain Aubrey Janion, who writes of Hawai'i's history, and Colonel Robert Doe, who taught it for years in schools and college, were friendly sources as was Virginia Wirtz, Director of the Maui Museum and Historical Society. Bob Fiddes was helpful in checking dates and events during World War II.

Mayor Elmer Cravalho encouraged me in the project, and Ron Youngblood assisted with information on county affairs. My neighbor, Armond Janssen, a longtime Maui resident and school man, loaned me several old books on Hawai'i, from his library.

Former students John and Mollie Geyer and Roberta Mercado helped with research and cheered me on. Charlie Keau was a knowledgeable guide to the archaeological sites on Maui and added to my understanding of Hawaiian ways.

The librarians at Wailuku and Maui Community College, as well as those at Kahului, were ever ready to render aid and encouragement to publish.

From Oahu, June Gutmanis, an experienced and able researcher and editor, came over to act as local editor for the first half of the book. She collected some of the illustrations for me and made copies of others, which I have used in this book. Dr. Kenneth Emory, Senior Anthropologist at the Bishop Museum in Honolulu, made many good suggestions over lunches at the Tapa Lanai at the Museum.

Mrs. Timberlake and her staff at the Bishop Museum Library; Mrs. Barbara Edkins, Librarian at the Peabody Museum of Salem; Ms. Dorota Starzecka, Assistant Keeper, the Ethnography Department of the British Museum; and Mr. G. Graham, Director of the Whitby Museum, Whitby, England, led me to materials on Hawaiian history, Cook's voyages, and British and American whaling that I would not otherwise have seen.

Special thanks go to Dot Russell, who patiently typed and retyped my manuscript, to Herb Kane for his handsome illustration done especially for the book's dust jacket, and to Anita Karl for the end-paper maps. Helen Toms first suggested using the files of the Lahaina Restoration Foundation. Larry Ikeda and other officials of the plantations generously filled my requests for information or illustrations. My son, Cummins E. Speakman III, was an ideal travelling companion and assistant as I completed research in England in June 1978.

Finally, to my brother-in-law, Harry Freeman Rice, and his wife Pat, who were responsible for my opportunities to study in England, and to my wife Julie, who held the fort, mahalo a nui loa.

This book is about people. Naturally, like most histories, the story is told in terms of leaders, but throughout I have tried to provide insights into the lives of the common people of Maui who make up the essential fabric of the island's life.

C.E.S. Jr.
Hale Kuau
Paia, Maui

October 1978

INTRODUCTION

In the centuries since Captain James Cook first arrived in the Hawaiian Islands, Maui has, in a sense, come full circle. The island's fascinating history begins with the politics of an ancient Hawaiian chiefdom struggling with internal civil conflict. Rich in resources—from the Ka'anapali coast to the slopes of Haleakala—Maui was seen as a valuable prize by its own people and those on neighboring islands.

Once the center of political and commercial life during the first decades of the Hawaiian Kingdom, Maui soon faded in importance as an increasingly Westernized culture turned from Lahaina to the deep-water port of Honolulu. For many years, Maui was ignored by the rising tide of foreigners in the Islands. At the dawn of the twentieth century, the rapid growth of the sugar and pineapple industries brought immigrants from as far away as the Philippines, China, Japan, and Portugal, changing the face of Maui's community indefinitely. Yet Maui managed to retain the rural qualities of island living that old-time residents still wistfully recall.

With the turn from agriculture to tourism, Maui continued to prosper economically. In the half-century since statehood, the island has blossomed into Hawai'i's leading alternative destination to the tourist war-zone of Waikiki. And with a watchful eye, Maui residents are making sure that their proud motto—"Maui no ka oi" (Maui is the best)—remains true throughout the years.

As the middle ground between highly developed O'ahu and the more rural neighbor islands of Moloka'i, Lana'i and Kaua'i, Maui has become the testing ground for a new vision of growth and development. At the brink of the twenty-first century, Maui began a calculated move away from environmentally-damaging tourism by attracting new industries to the island. Today, a growing population of transplants from the American Mainland, and descendents of plantation-era immigrants from around the world, debate the future of the Magic Isle. How Maui is perceived to have succeeded or failed in her attempts to join economic progress with a desirable "quality of life" will have a crucial role in the ongoing debate over Hawai'i's future.

CHAPTER I

THE BEGINNINGS: LAND AND PEOPLE

The various explorers from the West who discovered Pacific islands between the years 1500 and 1900 usually named them for friends, patrons, members of their crews, places in Europe, or even for some impressive characteristic of an island's terrain. In one case Captain James Cook, piloting his ships through a stormy sea, named a treacherous headland "Cape Foul Weather."

When Captain Cook first came upon the islands of Hawai'i he named them "The Sandwich Islands," in honor of the Earl of Sandwich, First Lord of the Admiralty and a patron of his Pacific voyages. However, there was no need to name these islands individually because each already bore a distinguishable name of Polynesian origin. Even the name Sandwich Islands did not persist, and the individual islands soon came to be known to the world by their ancient names.

Cook learned the true name of "the saddle shaped island" as he cruised off its northern shore in November 1778. On November 30, he wrote "Mowee" in the log of the *Resolution*, thus putting it down in writing for the first time in history. Maui is a name with very ancient roots, perhaps even antedating the most ancient Polynesian migrations.

MAUI, THE DEMIGOD

It is possible that Maui is simply a local place name, but it is widely believed to have derived from either the Polynesian demigod, *Maui-tikitiki-a-Taranga*, or an actual warrior-hero or great discoverer by that name. Stories of the demigod are recounted in all the Polynesian lands of the Pacific. "Priests, chiefs, and commoners tell stories about this versatile and capricious character who ranged over the sea, sky, earth, and underworld to defy the gods and enrich mankind."

Royalty of almost every Pacific land claims descent from Maui, and the royal family of Hawai'i was no exception–the last Hawaiian monarchs included Maui in their genealogies.

According to the many legends, Maui was a tricky demigod but, nevertheless, irresistible and blessed with extraordinary powers. These legends tell how Maui stole fire, raised the sky and snared the sun, fished up land and trapped winds, founded dynasties, changed landscapes, made useful inventions, terrified strong men, and rescued beautiful maidens. These fabulous deeds earned the culture-hero the name of *Maui-tinihanga*, "Maui-of-a-thousand-tricks."

Among all these powers, legend claims Maui as the founder of the Hawaiian Islands. He fished them up from the sea. In at least on Hawaiian legend he is credited with "redesigning" the first man by breaking him at the ankles, knees, and hips to create joints; then tearing the limbs loose from their webs of skin so that man could move about.

All the Polynesian legends agree that Maui arrested the sun's progress and regulated its course. Fornander, in tracing the origins of the Polynesian people, believed that the universality of the Maui legends points strongly to a common origin.

The best-known legend in Hawai'i with respect to Maui is the story of how he captured the sun in a net in the crater of Haleakala to prolong its passage over the island. The Maui legend of snaring the sun is found in numerous sources and almost as many different versions. Here is the version found in Wenkam's, *Maui, The Last Hawaiian Place*:

"When Maui lived on the island that bears his name he brought off his greatest Hawaiian exploit.

"The days were short on Maui Island. The gathering of bark and pounding of tapa required all day, and there was insufficient time remaining after pounding the wet tapa for it to dry before the sun dipped below the mountain rim. No time remained for the people to cook their food before dark and bring in the fishing nets they had laid out before dawn."

Maui resolved to snare the sun and halt its swift flight across the sky. He wove a cord from his sister's pubic hair, twisted it into throw lengths, and with these thrown over his shoulder, climbed to the summit of Haleakala, House of the Sun, and there awaited the light above the eastern rim.

When the Sun God stood full against the eastern sky, Maui lassoed him between the legs, a fighting technique that later Polynesian warriors would practice on their enemies. Maui beat the Sun God with a magic jawbone, permanently crippling him. The maimed sun now moves slowly across the sky and gives the people time to dry their tapa, bring in the nets, carefully extract the small fish caught in the mesh, and cook before dark.

Maui met a spectacular end. Seeking to gain immortality for himself and for the human race, he approached his beautiful but cruel ancestress, the great Hina of the Underworld. Maui found her asleep on her back. Believing that he could find the hidden source of life in her body and carry it back to mankind so that men might escape the indignity of death, Maui crawled between great Hina's thighs. "Maui's head disappeared, then his broad shoulders and chest. Hina did not stir. Finally only his legs stuck out…" Some enchanted birds, friends of Maui, who were watching, laughed. "Hina awoke, saw what was happening and, squeezing her legs together, crushed Maui."

This last trick of *Maui-tinihanga* was disastrous and, though it proved the end of Maui the demigod, the name lives on in the name of the island which some still find "irresistible."

AN ISLAND IS BORN

The Hawaiian island chain was created by lava flowing up from fissures in the sea bottom and coral building near the sea's surface. This process has been going on for at least twenty-five million years. Volcanic explosions of vast size created separate chains of volcanoes which, in some cases, joined to make one or more islands. Over these ages a continuous flow of lava helped tie them together with rock, then soil, and finally sand from the surrounding reefs.

In such a way the island of Maui was created. In the same way all along the great rift that had opened up in the Pacific's floor, other islands were formed. The second largest, Maui, was formed out of two volcanoes or volcanic complexes. These eventually became dormant and were joined into a single island, at first by the erosion of wind and rain and further by flows of lava.

There followed periods when the surrounding waters rose and fell. In this earth-building process, the islands of Kahoʻolawe, Lanaʻi, West Maui, East Maui, and Molokaʻi, at first separate volcanoes, became joined into one large island. Later, in stages which included the great submergence during the Olowalu stage, a two hundred and fifty foot stand of the sea, they became separate islands, and the steep valleys became deeply filled with alluvium.

At another, still later stage, East and West Maui were united once more in a period called Kahipa when the sea level fell about three hundred feet and Hana and Kaupo mud flows began to fill the canyons of East Maui. Finally, Maui took its present form (during the period called Waipio) when the sea stood at minus sixty feet, and dunes formed on the isthmus.

At some point in ancient times, seeds from other lands reached the island through storm-tossed birds, floating debris, or airborne spores, there to sprout upon newly formed shores. Soil building increased as vegetation became rooted and died to add organic strength to the volcanic sediments. Vast quantities of fresh water were brought to the islands by the Pacific trade winds, fertilizing the rich soil. Much of this beneficent moisture filtered through the porous rocks to be stored in underground reservoirs.

The island of Maui, with its two volcanoes, was still growing, unknown to the world of men, while great monuments arose in the Tigris and Euphrates valley and the rich culture of the Pharaohs blossomed in Egypt. In China, men were developing a highly sophisticated system of thought while others in Japan codified art principles that would enrich the world. Jesus of Nazareth pursued his ministry in Jerusalem, and Mohammed emerged from the Arabian desert with a new vision of Heaven.

These tiny specks of green in the northern Pacific Ocean slept in the sun—virginal, unimagined, a paradise ready to awaken.

THE POLYNESIANS DISCOVER HAWAI‘I

Toward the beginning of the Christian era two thousand years ago, a relatively short span of time in terms of the earth's age, a strong, sea-loving, tan-skinned people of Eastern Asia migrated to the Indonesian Archipelago, fanning out from there to the islands of the South Pacific. They settled briefly in Fiji, then migrated to Samoa, whence they are believed to have settled in New Zealand, Tahiti, the Marquesas, and later to have made the astounding voyages that brought them north across the empty seas to Hawai‘i. These people, the Polynesians, settled within the area which reaches from New Zealand to Easter Island to Hawai‘i and is known as the Polynesian Triangle. Very early in their migrations the Polynesians developed a high technical skill in boat building and navigation.

By the sixth century A.D., Polynesians had settled on the Hawaiian Islands, where they remained comparatively unknown for about five centuries, or until about 1000 A.D. Sometime during that century, several parties of fresh immigrants from the Society and Marquesas groups are believed to have arrived at the Hawaiian Islands, and for the space of five or six generations they maintained active intercourse with the islands far to the south, especially Tahiti.

No one knows just where the first discoverers, the legendary Menehune, landed. But there is a tradition that the second wave, the Ali‘i, found its first landing place at South Point on the island of Hawai‘i, while still other traditions point to landings at the Waipio Valley on Hawai‘i and on the island of Moloka‘i.

There is a tradition on Maui that the voyagers from Tahiti settled on the leeward side along the southern shore. This tradition is borne out by the name of an area of ancient ruins called Kahiki-nui, the word Kahiki being Hawaiian for Tahiti (or "horizon").

However, the line of great warrior chiefs of divine lineage descended from the Tahitians became established on the island of

Hawai'i, where oral genealogies and chants celebrated their exploits. These are the very first records we have of the island people, because they did not develop a written language.

Fornander speaks of the eleventh century as a period when "Polynesian folklore in all the groups becomes replete with heroic legends and songs of remarkable men, bold expeditions, great adventures and voyages to far-off lands." After this period, the intercourse of the Hawaiians with the Society Islands appears to have ceased, and no more is heard of these exploits except for the bare genealogical tree.

During the first century or two of the second period, intercourse with the distant southern homelands was maintained by means of the great Polynesian sailing canoes. These were sometimes over 100 feet long, double-hulled with large platforms and shelters. They were capable of sustaining sixty to eighty people with all their gear for voyages of 1,800 to 2,000 miles nonstop.

A century ago, Fornander himself saw one hull near South Point, Hawai'i, that measured 108 feet. But the art of making and navigating these great vessels seems to have declined around 1200 or 1300 A.D. when the Hawaiians became, for another 500 years, isolated from any further contacts with other lands.

RULING CHIEFS

One of the most famous chiefs in Hawaiian prehistory was Umi-a-Liloa ("son of Liloa") who, probably sometime during the sixteenth century or early seventeenth century, succeeded in uniting the districts of the Big Island of Hawai'i into a kingdom. Umi thus deserves the title, Ruling Chief, or Moi, a Hawaiian word which is generally translated in most histories by the English word "king", although king, strictly speaking, should be used only for the Kamehamehas whose progenitor united all the islands into a true kingdom.

While Umi ruled Hawai'i, a powerful chief on Maui achieved the unification of the districts of Maui by war. His name was

Piʻilani, and he gave his daughter in marriage to Umi on Hawaiʻi. Her name was Piʻikea and, because of her birth and her beauty, she became the principal and favorite wife of Umi.

The marriage of this high chiefess and the Moi of Hawaiʻi was a factor in the long peace which marked the reigns of these two famous ruling chiefs. "From the beginning of Umi's reign until he became old, there was continued peace with his father-in-law, Piʻilani, ruler of Maui, and with his chiefs. No battle was fought between the two kingdoms. After the death of Piʻilani, father of Piʻikea, trouble began with the heir of the kingdom."

THE SONS OF PIʻILANI

The great Maui chief had two sons, both born of a mother of the highest rank. The chief willed Maui to his eldest son, Lono-a-Piʻilani, but on the father's death the rivalry between the sons erupted into open hostility, and Kiha-a-Piʻilani, the younger, was forced to flee when Lono sought to kill him. While a refugee living incognito at Hana, Kiha fell in love with a young chiefess, Koleamoku, the daughter of the paramount chief of the Hana districts.

The legends tell of the meeting of Kiha and the fair chiefess at Hana Bay where the two came to enjoy the Ke-anini surf. Kiha, reared on Oʻahu, was a champion of the long surf at Waikiki, but the chief's daughter soon taught him how to master the short surf of the bay.

Kiha was filled with desire for the chiefess, although unaware that her father had promised her in marriage to the ruling chief, his brother Lono. Kolea fell deeply in love with the younger and more handsome Kiha and, on a day of perfect surfing, the youths rode exhilarated to the beach where they made love. Kolea "was determined to have him for a husband but her father was set against it because she was betrothed to the ruling chief..."

Nevertheless, the two were secretly married, and Kolea gave birth to a son. Lono immediately made war against his brother who, with his new wife, took refuge with his sister and her

husband, Umi, on the Big Island. Umi took the side of the younger brother, Kiha, and, after "the long peace," a bitter war between
Hawaiʻi and Maui was launched. Umi provided a vast fleet of war
canoes and many warriors, an invasion of Maui was set afoot, and
Lono was defeated.

The legend tells that on learning of the victory of Umi and
Kiha, Lono died of fright. The victors divided Maui, and the Hana
districts fell under the control of the chief of Hawaiʻi. Apparently,
Kiha and Kolea (along with Kumaka, his brave and faithful first
wife) "lived happily ever after," and became the ancestors of many
a Maui chieftain.

Kiha's name is forever preserved in Maui history as the build-
er of the Kiha-a-Piʻilani Highway which circles the western part of
the island and joins with the straight and smoothly paved highway
which was begun by ancient chiefs and finished by the Moi,
Piʻilani, the father. This part of the highway is the eastern roadway
running by way of Kaupo and through the crater. Remains of the
Piʻilani Highway are to be found today in some places but more
often have disappeared beneath the roadbed of the modern highway around the island, still called by its ancient name. The name is
also preserved in that of the great heiau at Hana, the Hale-o-Piʻilani
(or House of Piʻilani), itself as remarkable a monument as the highway.

Umi assisted in building the island roadway, and the friendship of the two ruling families continued to give the people of Maui
and Hawaiʻi another long period of peace. One of the most beautiful spots on Maui is the high place at Haiku called The Hill of Umi.
Maui, in this period, came to be called "The Haven of Piʻilani," and
the people of Maui were to look back with longing to this era in
their history, when the wars of the chiefs in the seventeenth and
eighteenth centuries became a painful burden on the land and its
people.

CHAPTER 2

THE HUNDRED YEARS' WAR
AND THE DYNASTY OF KE-KAU-LIKE

Historians sometimes speak of the seventeenth and eighteenth centuries in Hawaiian history as the period of the "hundred years' war" or wars. Around 1700, one chief, a descendant of the Piʻilani chiefs, established through war a powerful and united "kingdom" on Maui. His name was Ke-kau-like, "The Just." His sons fought over the succession briefly but continued to rule Maui for over half a century. For some time, they gave their people peaceful years, but during the last decades the island of Maui was devastated, and its people, especially the commoners, were living in poverty. By the end of the eighteenth century, even the chiefs were impoverished. Vancouver, when he visited King Ka-hekili of Maui in 1793, found that not even the king himself could supply his ships with provisions as the English moved along the southeast coast of Maui and anchored at Lahaina.

War seems to have been less predominant in Hawaiian antiquity—the very early period was that of long voyages, settlement, and survival, which took up the energies later devoted to hostilities. By tradition, the ruling aliʻi were inspired and gave the best laws, the *Kanawai Akua*, or God's Laws, to the priests, who in turn gave the laws to the chiefs. These latter had the duty to proclaim the laws and see that the commoners obeyed them. War was not a common affair.

The ancient battles appear to have been the affairs of the aliʻi. Fought according to long established rules of warfare, they seldom, if ever, involved the entire population. But for several centuries before Kamehameha conquered and killed the warring chiefs, the battles of the chiefs on the islands and between the islands periodically kept the people in turmoil. After 1778, the whole character of these wars changed as iron weapons and then firearms were introduced.

By the third decade of the eighteenth century, major battles for control of the islands were constantly in progress. Alapaʻi was the ruling chief of the island of Hawaiʻi. He sought to subdue Maui, was unsuccessful, and was counterattacked by the warrior king of Maui, Ke-kau-like, who raided the island of Hawaiʻi, killing many warriors and devastating the lands at Kona and Kohala, where he abused the country people. He cut down all the coconut trees at Kawaihae, another insulting act of war as coconut trees had very special significance for the Hawaiians. He slaughtered the people of Kohala, across the channel from Hana, seized their possessions, and returned to Maui.

Previous to these raids, Ke-kau-like had erected temple platforms dedicated to the gods of war in the Kaupo area, and it was there that he settled to make ready for further conquest of the Big Island.

"But God ordered it otherwise, for he was seized with a violent illness, or epilepsy, called, 'Eyes-drawn-heavenward' *(ka-maka-huki-lani)* which defied the skill of the doctors. Hence the succession of the land was settled at Kaupo, and Kamehameha-nui* was made ruler of the land of Maui."

Ke-kau-like, hearing that Alapaʻi was at Kohala preparing to attack Maui, was afraid and, though ill, fled in his double war canoe to West Maui. He sailed with his officers, war leaders, and his many wives and children along the leeward side of the island, some of his warriors and retinue traveling by land along the Piʻilani Highway. The fleet landed below Kula, and a litter was prepared for the dying king, who was carried overland to a place called Halekiʻi. There he died. The ashes of his flesh were placed in the waters of the ʻIao stream, which carried them to the mother sea whence he had come. His bones were hidden in the caves near the heiau. Ke-kau-like was the last of the Maui aliʻi to be interred at ʻIao.

"Alapaʻi sailed from Kohala with a great company of the chiefs of Hawaiʻi, his war leaders, warriors, and district chiefs… But when he landed at Mokulau in Kaupo and heard that Ke-kau-like was dying, he gave up all thought of war and wished only to meet Ke-kau-like and his (Alapaʻi's) sister the chief wife of Ke-kau-like. He had heard that Kamehameha-nui had been cho-

---

* Eldest son of Ke-kau-like; not to be confused with Kamehameha I, the conqueror.

sen ruler over Maui and he had no desire to make war on his sister's child."

Despite the support of Alapaʻi, a fratricidal battle for the succession to the Maui kingdom ensued. Another son of Ke-kau-like challenged his half brother. He was Ka-uhi.

For several years after Ke-kau-like's death, the war continued. A major battle took place at Honokowai in West Maui. The forces of Alapaʻi and the young Maui heir were badly mauled and withdrew. Another battle occurred in which the ruling chief of Oʻahu fought in alliance with Ka-uhi, the challenger. The hardest fighting happened at Puʻunene in the dry central plain of Maui. The slaughter was great on both sides, and a stalemate resulted in a peaceful settlement between the ruling chiefs.

Kamehameha-nui's rule of Maui was confirmed. He ruled the Maui kingdom for twenty-nine peaceful years. He had many wives and children, none of whom succeeded him. In his last illness while at Hana, he named his favorite brother, Ka-hekili-nui-ahu-manu ("The Thunder King"), as his heir. Kamehameha-nui's body lay at the heiau at Paukukalo, and later his remains were removed to the burial place of high chiefs on the island of Molokaʻi.

KA-HEKILI, LAST OF MAUI'S RULING CHIEFS

The Thunder King's reign over Maui lasted for about twenty-five years. He was the last of the traditional high, or "sacred," aliʻi to rule, and, though he ruled in peace for a time, his reign is notable for the bitter wars which culminated in his defeat by Kamehameha the Great in 1790 and his death on Oʻahu in 1794.

The fortunes and misfortunes of this warrior chief dominated the history of Maui, "the island between," during the last half of the eighteenth century. The story is complicated by the seesaw of war—war between Hawaiʻi and Maui, between Maui and Oʻahu—and by the complex battles within these islands between rival chiefs. Ka-hekili was in the thick of all these struggles even in old age, and before he lost the prize, the united kingdom, he had conquered

Moloka'i, Lana'i, O'ahu, and placed his brother Ka-'eo on Kaua'i as ruling chief. Hawai'i, alone, he failed to conquer. Although he tried on several occasions, he was repulsed each time.

The history of Ka-hekili's period is further complicated for the reader, especially one who does not know Hawaiian, by the names and locations of battles, the names of the chiefs and their battle leaders, their wives and children, and most of all by the close blood or adoptive relationships and marriage bonds between them. A partial family tree of the Maui royal family established by Ke-kau-like may help in understanding the blood connections but does not show what the real relationships were, as; among the ali'i, blood was not always thicker than water, and the most fierce battles of the eighteenth-century ruling chiefs transpired between close relatives.

THE WARRING CHIEFS

Ka-hekili's greatest enemy was the ruling chief of Hawai'i, Ka-lani-'opu'u, another fighting chief who, throughout his rule of the Big Island, sought again and again to conquer Maui. He never took the whole island but succeeded in taking over the Hana districts for a period of about twenty years and came back for several brief interludes and raids after that.

After Ka-lani-'opu'u's death, and the death of his sons, Kamehameha became the chief on Hawai'i and the mortal enemy of the aging Ka-hekili.

During the early, peaceful years of Ka-hekili's reign, or perhaps before, his sister, the High Chiefess Ka-lola, became the principal wife of Ka-lani-'opu'u, who initiated the long war between these brothers-in-law by "mercilessly beating the people of Kaupo with clubs" and otherwise mistreating them. Ka-hekili retaliated by taking the fortress of Ka'uiki, killing its defenders, and driving out the Hawaiian chiefs who had so long controlled the districts of Hana, Kipahulu, and Kaupo.

Around 1775, the Hawaiian king returned with his war canoes and raided the Hana districts but was defeated at Kaupo.

This persistent chief, known as an indomitable warrior, was never to gain control of all Maui. However, in the following year, he mounted a full-scale attack, took Hana, and proceeded with his fleet of war canoes to Makena and then to Maʻalaea.

THE BATTLE OF THE SAND HILLS

"This is the house of your god; open the sluice gate that the fish may enter." These were the words of the high priest to Ka-hekili at the dedication of the war heiau at Wailuku as the king prepared for invasion from Hawaiʻi. It meant, "The war god is in his house and favors your victory; fall back to let the enemy into your net and kill them like fish."

Ka-hekili deployed his forces on either side of the plain, hidden in the sand hills above the heiau. Ka-lani-ʻopuʻu sent his elite squadron toward Wailuku to spearhead the attack. These were the crack troops called Alapa, consisting of 800 men, "all expert spear-point breakers, every one of whose spears went straight to the mark like arrows...Across the plains...their helmets...shone like crescents in the sun." All were eager with the thought that the Alapa were soon to drink the cool waters of Wailuku.

Ka-hekili was lying in wait for them. The high priest said, "The fish have entered the sluice; draw the net." The battle took place to seaward of the sand hills near Wailuku. The Alapa were defeated in a terrible slaughter. When the net was drawn only two men escaped to bear the awful news to Ka-lani-ʻopuʻu, who was taken with a chill and mournfully wailed for the dead.

He consulted his war leaders, one of them his favorite, Kamehameha, and the remaining fighters. They said, "Tomorrow we will drink the waters of Wailuku and rest in the shade of Hekuawa."

Ka-hekili and his ally and nephew, the ruling chief of Oʻahu, prepared another fish net, and again the fish swam into it. Ka-hekili's men rose before dawn and took their stand in the sand hills, some toward the Waikapu turn. The invading force from Hawaiʻi found a divided front from which the spears poured down on them "like a swift rainstorm." The terrified soldiers were surrounded and fled.

Ka-lani-'opu'u, seeing his men surrounded and facing total defeat and death, asked his wife, Ka-lola, to intercede with her brother Ka-hekili. She refused but suggested that their son, the young chief of divine rank, Kiwala'o, be sent to his uncle to sue for peace.

As Kiwala'o approached Wailuku, garbed in his splendid red and yellow feather cloak* and helmet, the Maui soldiers fell to the ground on both sides in deference to his rank and because of the severe tabu which required prostration to avoid facing the sacred back of a chief. The Maui defenders reluctantly observed the kapu.

Ka-hekili, seeing his approach, "turned his face upward (a sign of a favorable reception)," Kiwala'o entered and sat on the chest of his uncle**, who embraced him. A truce was arranged and Ka-hekili said, "'Let live! Let the battle cease!' and he asked, 'Where is my sister (Ka-lola)?' Ka-hekili then sent food to his brother-in-law and the chiefs became reconciled. But Ka-lani-'opu'u's was a feigned friendship."

Only a few years later, the Hawai'i king returned to war on Maui, killing many people at Kaupo and sailing on to Lahaina. Ka-hekili again prepared for battle, and fighting took place near Ka'anapali. In the battle, the warrior chief Kamehameha distinguished himself for bravery and skill in war. The Hawai'i chiefs then carried the war to the island of Lana'i, which was cruelly devastated. The food ran out and Ka-lani-'opu'u set sail along the north shore of Maui, raiding the Hamakua villages as he approached Hana.

It was at Wailua-iki or at Hana that Ka-lani-'opu'u and the remnants of his fighting forces first saw the strange "floating heiaus of Lono," the ships of the Cook expedition. It was November 1778.

---

* The Kiwala'o Cloak: He may have worn the very cloak which later belonged to Kamehameha and hangs in the main hall of the Bishop Museum, Honolulu.

** Fathers of children of higher rank received them publicly in this way as it was a mark of respect for rank to keep the child's head higher than that of the father. The phrase is quoted from Kamakau's book, *Ruling Chiefs of Hawai'i*.

CHAPTER 3

THE FATEFUL CONTACT: 1778-1779

*It was not the Hawaiians as a people who deified Cook,
but the priests of Lono. It was not the Hawaiians as a people who killed him, but the chiefs and their fighting men,
devotees of Ku, the war god, acting as protectors of their
ruler, Ka-lani-'opu'u…*

– Gavan Daws, *Shoal of Time.*

For two hundred years before Captain James Cook found Hawai'i, the Spanish had been crossing the Pacific. They made regular crossings from Acapulco in Mexico to the Philippines, and there are some good reasons for believing that the Hawaiian Islands were known to them. However, final proof of this is lacking.

A chart captured from a Spanish vessel by the British Lord Anson in 1743 showed islands situated ten degrees off the longitude of Hawai'i. The mistake in charting could have been caused by the Equatorial currents, then unknown, but more probably it resulted from the inaccuracy of sixteenth- and seventeenth-century navigating instruments. Approximate latitude could be determined with relative ease, but at that time no shipboard instrument capable of finding longitude had been invented.

La Pérouse, Maui's first European visitor, followed the Spanish charts and, finding nothing where in 1542 the Spanish navigator Juan Gaetano was supposed to have found islands, sailed straight on to make his Hawaiian landfall. La Pérouse, a great admirer of Cook, still gave the latter credit for the discovery but was apparently convinced that Gaetano's islands were, in fact, the Hawaiian Archipelago.

Even more convincing are the journals of Vancouver's voyage, which indicate the general belief on board his ships that the islands called Los Majos on the Spanish chart were, indeed, the windward islands of the Hawaiian chain.

Finally, according to the English missionary William Ellis, there was a tradition among the chiefs on Hawai'i of landings by white men well before Cook arrived. One story was repeated by Hawaiians whom Ellis met on his hike around the Big Island in 1822. It told of a boat which had no sail but instead a canopy of white tapa containing several white men, landing at Kealakekua Bay. Here the crew disembarked and later went up the mountain, where they lived for a time, eventually departing in their boat. Other traditions persist including that of a Spanish shipwreck on Maui's shore. "Be that as it may,"* Cook was the first navigator to make known to Europe the existence of the Hawaiian group.

THE FATEFUL CONTACT

The great English explorer, Captain James Cook, had already made two voyages in the Pacific, had explored its furthest reaches, had discovered lands previously unknown to the West, and had charted for the first time islands, bays, rivers, reefs, and coastlines of this greatest of all oceans. On his third, and last, voyage Cook sighted the Hawaiian chain.

Sailing north from the Society Islands in H.M.S. *Resolution*, his flagship, accompanied by H.M.S. *Discovery*, Cook sighted the island of O'ahu and then Kaua'i on January 18, 1778. He believed that this would probably rank as the most important of his many distinguished discoveries in the Pacific.

Cook made landings on Kaua'i and on Ni'ihau, trading with the natives and replenishing fresh water supplies before continuing his voyage in search of a northwest passage from the Pacific coast of America to the Atlantic.

During the summer of 1778, Cook searched the edge of the Arctic ice without finding a passage. He had the choice of spending the winter of 1778 at the Russian outpost of Petro-pavlovsk, Kamchatka, finding a haven on the lower part of the American

---

* A favorite phrase of Captain Cook which he frequently wrote in his earlier logbooks.

northwest coast, or returning to the Sandwich Islands which he had visited at the beginning of the year.

Cook decided to winter in the Sandwich Islands. His officers and men were exhausted, the ships were in very poor condition, especially the *Resolution*, which was leaking badly.

Cook, himself, was tired and looked forward to refreshing his crews and refitting his ships among the Hawaiian people whom he had already recognized as Polynesians.*

He also believed that there were other islands in the chain which remained to be discovered, and he planned further exploration and charting of the islands at which he had so very briefly touched in January. To winter in the Sandwich Islands was a logical decision. It was also a fateful one.

THE MOWEE LANDFALL, NOVEMBER 26-30, 1778

Passing through some of the worst storms encountered during any of his voyages, Cook steered for the Sandwich Islands. During a storm on November 2 the two ships lost sight of each other, and the *Resolution* had to lie to. When rejoined by the *Discovery*, Captain Charles Clerke reported to Cook that the main tack on the *Discovery* had fallen, killing one man and injuring two or three others.

The weather improved. Then, one last northerly gale on November 19 tore the *Resolution's* main topsail, just repaired, to pieces. The temperature rose steadily as they steered first east and then south, "the men sitting on deck sewing old sails, putting old rigging into order, and working up junk:** the stores were aired, the carpenters repaired the boats; all, no doubt, thought of joys to come." They remembered the alluring views of Kaua'i glimpsed in January and the pleasant Polynesian people encountered there.

It was November 25, 1778. That morning the latitude of Cook's ships put him a degree south of his Kaua'i anchorage at

---

* From 1768, when Cook first sailed to Tahiti, the Polynesian islanders, referred to in the eighteenth century as "Indians of the South Seas," became his friends and a very real part of his life. (From Barrow, *Capt. Cook in Hawaii, 1976*.)

** Junk is remnants of old cable, cut up to make points, mats, gaskets, sennit, etc. on board ship.

Waimea Bay, while his longitude was about four degrees to the east. At daybreak, November 26, 1778, Maui was seen for the first time by Europeans.

Captain Cook wrote in the logbook of H.M.S. *Resolution*:

> In the evening, we joined; and at midnight brought to. At daybreak, next morning, land was seen extending from South South East to West. We made sail, and stood for it. At eight, it extended from South East half South, to West; the nearest part two leagues distant. It was supposed that we saw the extent of the land to the East, but not to the West. We were now satisfied, that the group of the Sandwich Islands had been only imperfectly discovered; as those of them which we had visited in our progress Northward, all lie to the leeward of our present station.
>
> In the country was an elevated saddle hill, whose summit appeared above the clouds. From this hill, the land fell in a gentle slope, and terminated in a steep rocky coast, against which the sea broke in a dreadful surf. Finding that we could not weather the island, I bore up, and ranged along the coast to the Westward. It was not long before we saw people on several parts of the shore, and some houses and plantations. The country seemed to be both well wooded and watered; and running streams were seen falling into the sea in various places.

Cook's position that first day was approximately three miles off Kahului. Trading began at once as several hundred persons came out in canoes (Cook observed "five or six hundred persons," some of them swimming alongside).

On the second day off Maui, November 27, Cook wrote at length recording the ships' movements, the trade with the people, and the first sighting of the island of Moloka'i:

Seeing some canoes coming off to us, I brought to. As soon as they got along-side, many of the people, who conducted them, came into the ship, without the least hesitation. We found them to be of the same nation with the inhabitants of the islands more to leeward, which we had already visited; and, if we did not mistake them, they knew of our having been there. Indeed, it rather appeared too evident; for these people had got amongst them the venereal distemper; and, as yet, I knew of no other way of its reaching them, but by an intercourse with their neighbours since our leaving them.

We got from our visitors a quantity of cuttle-fish, for nails and pieces of iron. They brought very little fruit and roots; but told us that they had plenty of them on their island, as also hogs and fowls. In the evening, the horizon being clear to the Westward, we judged the Westernmost land in sight to be an island,* separated from that off which we now were. Having no doubt that the people would return to the ships next day, with the produce of their country, I kept plying off all night, and in the morning stood close in shore. At first, only a few of the natives visited us; but toward noon, we had the company of a good many, who brought with them bread-fruit, potatoes, tarro, or eddy roots, a few plantains, and small pigs; all of which they exchanged for nails and iron tools.

The Captain had already published three basic regulations for the conduct of his crew. Private trade with the local people was forbidden. This was an old, familiar rule and was necessary for the ships' provisioning and also because the articles which the ships now possessed for trade were in very short supply.

The second regulation was a new one. Cook ordered that no firearms whatever be carried out of the ship, either by officers or men, and that care be taken to keep the natives ignorant of the method of charging "such as we may be under a necessity to make use of."

* It was the island of Moloka'i.

The third order treated of disease. It was well known that Unalaska had been a great encouragement to "the Venereal"; some days before, all the men had been examined by the surgeons; the complaints remained. Cook was specific: "…in order to prevent as much as possible the communicating this fatal disease to a set of innocent people," no woman was to be admitted on any pretense to the ship without the Captain's permission; any man party to such an entry would be punished; any man having the disease or under suspicion of having it, who lay with a woman, would be severely punished; no suspected person would be allowed on shore on any pretense whatever.

After reading out these orders to his assembled crew, Cook made what Lieutenant James King called "a sensible speech" reinforcing them. He had taken the same precautions in January at Kaua'i, yet now among the first people to come aboard from Maui, Cook found melancholy evidence that his efforts there had been unsuccessful. "Or could it be that, after all, in the islands of the Pacific Ocean there were original roots of the malady? Some men tried to make themselves believe so. Cook did not. The island women certainly seemed to carry no fear in their handsome bosoms; repulsed from the ships, they were highly indignant, and the words they shouted were unambiguously words of abuse."

The villagers came out to look and touch the "floating heiaus," to marvel at the abundance of iron, and to bargain. They were excited but friendly, and they seemed to understand the principle of trading very well. Cook observed their honesty and rewarded the occupants of a canoe which rescued the unfortunate cat of the *Resolution*. This ship's cat, an animal unknown to the Hawaiians, fell overboard and was picked up, still alive, astern of Cook's ship. He presented the rescuers with an iron adze, a very valuable item indeed.

THE KING OF MOWEE OFFERS HIS ALOHA

During the day, Cook made no attempt to land but stood close in shore, trading. Ka-hekili was at Wailuku preparing his forces for further battle in case Ka-lani-'opu'u should attack once again. Early in the morning of November 26, he looked out to sea, astonished at the approach of the tall ships and at first fearful of what they might mean to him and his people. Ka-hekili, however, was not totally unprepared for this event. His brother Ka-'eo was ruling Chief of Kaua'i and his close ally, and the Maui chief was privy to all the details of Cook's visit to the leeward islands ten months earlier. The King boldly decided to pay an official call.

The royal canoe was prepared, the Maui chiefs assembled and were invited to act as the King's paddlers, and offerings were made at the heiau. Ka-hekili put on his crested feather helmet and his most splendid royal cloak made of the brilliant feathers of the *i'iwi* and the *mamo*, red and yellow, probably inherited from his father, Ke-kau-like, and handed down to him by his brother who ruled Maui before him.*

The ten chiefs who manned the canoe wore capes of red feathers, as only the highest or ruling chiefs could possess the long cloaks.

As the King's canoe approached, it was seen to be heading for the *Discovery* rather than the flagship *Resolution*. Perhaps the *Discovery* at that moment was closer inshore than the *Resolution*. The commoners fell back as the splendid royal canoe drew near. The officers and men on board the *Discovery* watched fascinated from her decks. One of them, David Samwell, Surgeon's Mate, wrote "In the afternoon, Kaheekere (Ka-hekili) King of Mowee, and Morotai, came out to *Discovery* with a large train dressed in red feather cloaks. They sang in concert like the Oteihitians." Ka-hekili was received ceremoniously by Captain Charles Clerke and ushered into his cabin where names were exchanged in friendship and reciprocal presents were given, among them, the Kings' cloak.

Samwell thought the King unprepossessing, though colorful in his regalia, and was curious to observe that his head was tattooed in half circles on one side, his hair cut away on the sides leaving a crest on top. The Samwell journal also mentions seeing two iron skewers or daggers, the sight of which again raised questions in the officers' minds of a possible Spanish visit. In another of the English journals, that of James Burney, a chief with Ka-hekili is described as crossing his fingers when the daggers were observed and pointing toward shore. This

---

* The cloak may be one of those exhibited in the Cook collections in the British Museum, London, or the Bishop Museum, Honolulu.

caused further speculation that a cross may have been erected there, but no further information was elicited.

Before nightfall, Ka-hekili was carried ashore, and Cook took the ships out to sea during the night, returning the next day to trade for provisions which now began to appear more plentifully. Still making no attempt to land, Cook briefly sought to round Maui's western end, but winds and tides were against him, and he turned eastward along the Hamakua (north) coast of Maui going close inshore by day and standing off again at night.

The Captain sadly realized the impossibility of keeping the seamen and the Hawaiian women apart, and soon the women were coming aboard in large numbers. The trading, too, was opened to private bargaining, though the replenishment of ships' stores took precedence.

COOK MEETS THE PRESENT AND FUTURE KING

Four days after the visit of Ka-hekili off central Maui, the ships, cruising east, were approached by another important visitor. This royal personage was to welcome Cook officially at Kealakekua Bay many weeks later, but on November 30 he appeared in a large double canoe off Hana (some say it was off Keanae-Wailua) accompanied by his chiefs and retinue, was "handed up the side with great care by his followers, partly because of the feebleness to which he had been reduced by excessive drinking of kava, manifested in his scab-encrusted skin and red-inflamed eyes." Cook noted that he was observant and good natured as he visited the Captain's cabin, and presented Cook with two small pigs; Cook did not know then that this was the ruling chief of another island.

But perhaps the most important visitor was the young chief who was destined to conquer and unite all the islands. Kamehameha came aboard with his uncle, Ka-lani-'opu'u,* with whose permission he spent the night aboard the *Resolution*. Kamehameha was accompanied by other young chiefs, and the aging king, returning

---

* Cook heard his name as 'Terreeoboo.' It was, of course, none other than Ka-hekili's arch enemy, Ka-lani-'opu'u, still on Maui, still at war, and still hoping to take the rich prize from his brother-in-law and avenge the humiliating defeats suffered in his Maui campaigns.

to shore, sent back a large double canoe for them which was tied up to the *Resolution's* stern for the night.

The future king observed the modern weapons with the closest interest. It was his first meeting with westerners and western technology. He observed well, for they were to be of crucial significance in the success of this ambitious and capable chief in establishing a kingdom in Hawai'i.

That last day of November 1778 was an eventful day in the history of Maui and the Islands. Captain Cook and King Ka-lani-'opu'u met for the first of many times, exchanging names and pledging friendship, though neither one of them was quite sure just who the other was. Kamehameha, described by Lieutenant King as about twenty-five years of age and "of savage mien," spent that day and the night aboard the *Resolution,* probably not sleeping but observing with his quick mind everything that was to be seen on board. On that same evening before the sun went down, Cook saw the island of Hawai'i, another "first" in his remarkable Pacific discoveries. It was to be his last.

KEALAKEKUA BAY

As the first day of December 1778 ended, the English ships were close up to the northern side of the island, which Cook was told was called "O' why' he". The next morning revealed high mountains with snowy summits, pieces of white cloth flying on shore, canoes coming out flying white streamers; Cook flew his ensign in reply. The paddlers of the canoes, at first rather shy, soon understood the possibilities of trade; and by evening Cook had determined to ply further to windward around this island.

The hopes of officers and crew for escaping the long confinement of the ships rose as they drew close in to the new land. But it was to be another seven weeks of cruising off and on; Cook bringing the ships in toward land only when they needed supplies. There was quite a lot of bad weather and once or twice the ships were in danger of going on the rocks.

It was during this long and tiresome search for an anchorage, that Cook for the first and only time came close to facing mutiny. The cause of discontent centered around the Captain's decision to substitute for the crews' daily ration of grog (rum and water) a "strong decoction of sugar-cane beer." Cook had made this from a batch of cane obtained from the Maui people. He judged it to be good and nutritious as well as anti-scorbutic. The ships' officers drank it and assured the Captain that it was good and, with an eye to conserving the spirits for the return to the colder shores of the north, Cook ordered the substitution.

The men refused to touch the stuff and demanded their grog. Cook was annoyed, especially when he was handed a "very mutinous letter" of protest from the sailors.*

It was apparently a very tense situation as neither the men nor the officers fully understood the Captain's decision to keep the ships at sea for those long weeks and he did not share his reasons with them.

But the matter blew over and on the evening of December 18 in a heavy squall followed by a calm the *Resolution* was swept dangerously close to the shore off Cape Kumukahi. A breeze came up which barely enabled the ship with all sails set to clear the land. Just at the peak of anxiety ropes gave way and the main topsail and both topgallant sails were rent in two. "It was as narrow an escape as Cook ever had from losing his ship."

After another whole month of cruising around the island of Hawai'i, trading for hogs and vegetables as needed, Cook found his anchorage. A bay appeared in the morning of January 15, 1779, and Bligh was sent with a boat from each ship to find an anchorage.

"The evening brought back Bligh reporting good anchorage, fresh water, peaceable and friendly people. Cook could defer no longer. Next morning, 17 January, he stood into Kealakekua Bay and anchored, a quarter of a mile from the shore, in 13 fathoms of water." No less than a thousand canoes were counted surrounding the ships with perhaps as many as ten thousand people in them or in the water.

---

* The letter is mentioned by King and others but has never been found.

The first persons of importance to receive Captain Cook were the priests led by the high priest Kao who insisted on putting the Captain through elaborate religious ceremonies at the heiau on the shore. Provisioning and repairs went on; an abundance of women flocked on board the ships, and two handsome chiefs, Palea and Kanina, cooperated to control the people crowding about the ships and on their decks.

No other civil authority appeared until January 24 when a solemn kapu was pronounced over the entire Bay. This kept people in their houses, canoes on shore, and the ships short of vegetables. The next evening a long line of large sailing and paddling canoes came round the north point. King Terreeoboo (Ka-lani-'opu'u) came aboard the *Resolution* for the second time. To Cook's great surprise, he recognized the same tall, emaciated, red-eyed, but amiable king who had visited him off Maui two months earlier.

After visiting, introducing his queen and two young sons, and receiving presents, he retired to his town of Kaawaloa to sleep. The kapu was off the Bay, and the ladies—"our old Sweethearts," in Samwell's phrase—were restored to their lovers.

A ROYAL RECEPTION

Ka-lani-'opu'u's formal welcome took place the next day, a splendid water procession consisting of three large double canoes—in the first, the King and his chiefs richly attired in red and yellow feather cloaks and in the second canoe, Kao and the priests escorting four images of the gods made of feather-covered basket work with features of dogs' teeth, eyes of pearl-oyster shell.

They circled the ships, then landed ashore where Cook followed them. On their meeting, the King took off his own feather cloak, threw it round the Captain's shoulders and placed on his head a handsome *mahiole* or crested feather helmet. Into Cook's hand he gave a royal feather standard or *kahili*. At the Captain's feet Ka-lani-'opu'u laid half a dozen more cloaks, a truly regal gift.

The King returned with Cook to dine on the *Resolution* and to receive presents in his turn. These included a complete tool chest, a valuable present in the King's eyes.

The friendliest relations existed between the Hawaiians and their visitors. There were exhibitions of Hawaiian boxing, fireworks ordered by Cook; "A constant exchange of good offices and mutual little acts of friendship obtained among us," Trevenen wrote.

Thus January passed, and the time for departure drew near. On February 4, the ships sailed out of the Bay with an escort of canoes. Despite signs that the visitors had strained the islanders' resources and even "worn out their welcome" there were tears and promises of a return. Cook set out to explore the leeward side of Maui, to further explore the islands seen a year before, and to take on supplies of good water at the old watering place at Kaua'i. This would be needed as they headed north once more to seek a passage to the Atlantic.

COOK'S DEATH, FEBRUARY 14, 1779

They were back at Kealakekua Bay in a week. After a series of strong gales off Kawaihae, the head of the *Resolution's* foremast was found to be badly sprung. It would have to be taken out before it could be repaired and return to the Bay was the only viable alternative. Cook gave the order and the ships sailed again into the harbor at Kealakekua, which this time was completely deserted. Terreeoboo had placed a kapu on all traffic in the Bay.

The British missed the excitement of their previous tumultuous welcome but did not sense any great change at first. However, it became clear that a tension existed in the relations with the ordinary Hawaiians although the chiefs and priests and especially the King were as friendly as ever. A series of incidents included several cases of thievery, which was unusual, and a skirmish over the boat of one of the chiefs with stones flying. The death and burial of one of the seamen below the heiau was observed with both Hawaiian and Christian ceremonies. There were indications that the more intimate relations of the visitors and their hosts had led the latter to view these men of Lono as less than divine, and certainly not to be feared any longer.

Work on the mast continued at the heiau under the supervision of Lieutenant King and was almost completed when, on the morning of February 14, it was suddenly observed that the big cutter belonging to the *Discovery* had been stolen during the night. Between 6 and 7 A.M. Captain Cook decided that the only way to get this very important and necessary piece of equipment back was to bring Ka-lani-'opu'u on board and hold him hostage until the cutter was returned. This had worked for Cook under similar circumstances on other islands and he set forth to find the King. Meanwhile, he ordered Captain Clerke to see that the Bay was immediately closed off by armed men in the ships' remaining boats.

He took nine of his marines with him and ordered them (for the first time since his arrival) to load their muskets with ball. In his own double-barrelled musket he loaded first small shot, then ball.

Finding Terreeoboo asleep at his village, he wakened him and invited him to visit the flagship. The King, unsuspecting, accepted and his two young boys ran ahead to jump in Cook's boat for another of their almost daily visits to the ships.

As the Captain escorted the King to the boats, a very large crowd collected on the beach (later estimated to be a thousand people). Terreeoboo's queen, the boys' mother, suddenly became agitated, ran to the King and begged him not to go with Cook. The crowd moved in closer, and the marines formed a line at the water's edge facing them. Some of the attendants pushed the King to a sitting position where he remained looking about with utmost confusion.

The Hawaiians were arming themselves with spears and stones, many had daggers, some of them the iron pahoas obtained from the English.

Molesworth Phillips, who commanded the marines, was with Cook and observed at that moment "an artful rascal of a priest... singing and making a ceremonious offering of a coconut to the Captain and Terreeoboo to divert their attention from the manoeuvres of the surrounding multitude."

At that moment, Cook still had the initiative and there was nothing to stop him and Phillips moving down to the boats and taking off the marines. This they both decided to do and Cook began walking slowly down.

At that moment, news of firing at the other end of the Bay and the resulting death of a popular chief, who was in a canoe seeking to break out of the Bay, was received by the crowd and spread like wildfire. This news "was enough to carry the crowd over the borderline of excitement into attack."

The next moment, Cook, threatened by one of the mob with a dagger and a stone, fired one barrel, loaded with small shot, at this person. Beaglehole, Cook's most eminent biographer, believed that it was at this moment that "the strained cord of his temper snapped, (and) he lost the initiative."

> The man being protected by his heavy war mat, the shot did not damage–except that it further enraged the Hawaiians. Kalei'opu'u's (sic) young son in the pinnace was frightened and was put ashore; but even then the men in the boats saw no particular reason for alarm. In the next second the wave broke. A chief attempted to stab Phillips, stones were hurled, a marine was knocked down, Cook fired his other barrel, loaded with ball, and killed a man; Phillips fired, there was a general attack, Cook ordered the marines to fire, and the boats joined in unordered. Phillips had time to reload his musket. The overwhelmed marines did not. Cook shouted 'Take to the boats!', an order hardly necessary, as the unfortunate and ill-trained men were already scrambling into the water and towards the pinnace, 'totally vanquish'd', as Phillips said. Phillips himself was knocked down by a stone and stabbed in the shoulder, shot his assailant dead and managed to get to the pinnace; and then out of it again to save the life of a drowning man. In all this tumult he lost sight of Cook. The men in the pinnace saw Cook's last moments. He was close to the lava edge

waving to the boats to come in when he was hit from
behind with a club; while he staggered he was stabbed in
the neck, or the shoulder, with one of the iron daggers–
a blow which, not in itself fatal, was enough to fell him,
strong as he was, face down in the water. There was a
great shout, and a rush to hold him under and finish
him off with daggers and clubs. The pinnace had gone
in as close to the shore as possible to rescue the flounder-
ing marines; the launch had not– Williamson, that
strange man incomprehensibly mistaking the meaning
of Cook's wave, had even moved further out. The over-
loaded pinnace pulled off, the cutter came round and
fired til she was recalled: the Resolution, hearing the
uproar and the firing, and seeing, whatever might be the
meaning of it all, that there was trouble on shore, fired
those of her own four-pounders that could be brought
to bear. It seems that the crowd had retired somewhat,
and there was a space of time enough to reclaim bodies.
The men in the boats may have been shocked out of all
awareness of this. Leaving the dead, Cook and four
marines, where they lay, the boats rowed back in silence
to the ships; and the ships fell silent.

In the affray, the ships' cannon had fired into the mob and
among the sixteen or seventeen Hawaiians killed were four chiefs,
two of them who had been good friends to the ships.

Captain Charles Clerke, who immediately succeeded to command of the expedition, although a sick man himself, showed remarkable level-headedness. Clerke ruled out vengeance which could have
led to further disaster but it was not possible to maintain complete
control. There was skirmishing around the heiau where the mast of the
Resolution was laid up for repairs. Nevertheless, Lieutenant King succeeded in returning the mast to the ship without further incident. A
few guns were fired but there was no assault on the canoes and some
trading was resumed. Women continued to come out to the ships or
to remain on board overnight.

To try to get back the bodies of Cook and the four marines, King and Burney were sent ashore in the boats. The people discarded their weapons when they saw that the English carried a flag of truce. The old priest Kao swam out and informed Clerke that the body of Cook had been carried up the cliff side and gave some hints as to what the chiefs had done with the body.

Under pressure from Captain Clerke and the English officers, the remains of their Captain were finally returned. He had been given the treatment accorded the highest chiefs of Hawai'i, his flesh stripped from the bones and burned, the hands and feet preserved with salt. Ka-lani-'opu'u had the bones although it is clear that he, the good friend of Cook, was not implicated in his death.

After some delay, the bones, including the skull,* and the feet and hands, were delivered to Captain Clerke in a bundle wrapped in a black and white feather cloak. The hands were recognized as Cook's by the deep scar on his right hand which he had suffered from an exploding powder-horn on the Newfoundland coast.

The remains were put in a coffin and late in the day of February 21, 1779, "amid all the marks of naval grief, flags at half mast, crossed yards and half-minute guns, they were sunk in the waters of the bay."

Ka-lani-'opu'u sent one of his young sons aboard with presents to make peace and to collect a red and green cloak promised to him before Cook's death.

Two hundred years after Cook made known the Hawaiian Islands to the Western world little is known of what the reactions of the Hawaiians were to that first experience. In the absence of written records, it is difficult, if not impossible, to know what the Hawaiians thought. Evidences of the disease were palpable, yet, for many decades after, Cook was revered by the Hawaiians. Records were compiled from oral sources long years after the events and, as Hawai'i became more deeply involved in the turmoil of war, a spiritual, cultural, and social decline took place which was in part a result of influences introduced during and after the first fateful contact which led to the opening of the Islands to the outside world.

THE VOYAGE CONTINUES

The departure on February 22 from Kealakekua was accompanied by deep gloom not only among Cook's men but among the Hawaiians who would long remember him. Clerke followed the original plan, visiting other islands, seeking more water and sea stores, and settling the positions of the islands between Hawai'i and Kaua'i. Lieutenant John Gore, an American from Virginia, took Clerke's place as Commander of the *Discovery*, and second in command of the expedition.

Clerke intended to explore Maui further, but adverse winds were encountered. Cruising along the dry and uninviting coast of Kaho'olawe, he moved again toward the Maui shore, finally coming close in to Lahaina, where Thursday, February 25 was spent tacking off and on and trading with the canoes which came out to the ships. Intermittent winds and calms prevented a landing, and the course was set around Lana'i, then northward to pass close to the eastern tip of Moloka'i, where plantations were seen and six or eight canoes came off, though none of them had anything to trade, and the men were described as "very far removed from the ali'i." Samwell reported "many sharks about; we killed three or four."

By February 27, Clerke was noting the steep ridges and valleys of windward O'ahu, and February 28 the *Resolution* and *Discovery* came to anchor in Waimea Bay on O'ahu's north shore. Here, seven Hawaiian girls from Kealakekua were put ashore reluctantly. Samwell wrote "they were well pleased with their position aboard ship and would willingly (have gone) with us to England." When Clerke landed, he was greeted by a vast number of natives who prostrated themselves. He motioned them to rise. A chief came forward offering a hog, and brisk trading began. Taro, hogs, and other provisions were traded, but, the water proving brackish, Clerke decided to continue on to Kaua'i. The Captain and his landing party from the *Resolution* were the first known foreigners to set foot on the island of O'ahu.

---

* Several sources have recorded the tradition among the Hawaiians which says that Kamehameha kept Cook's hair. The scalp with the ears attached, but the hair cut off, was returned with the other remains.

At first, the Cook expedition was not well received on this second visit at Kaua'i, and it was learned at once by Lieutenant King, who led the first party ashore, that news of Cook's death had already reached there. Skirmishes over water casks and muskets snatched from the marines led to Lieutenant King's shooting a man in self defense. Nevertheless, communication continued, and those trading about the ships were friendly.

The whole atmosphere changed when the High Chiefess of Kaua'i came aboard with her consort. This was none other than Ka-'eo, the chief from Maui, Ka-hekili's brother. It was his son, Ka-umu-ali'i, the "gentle king" who welcomed the first missionaries to Kaua'i many years later. The ruling chiefess proved to be a generous friend, sending a canoe-load of presents to Clerke after he had left Kaua'i for Ni'ihau to obtain a supply of yams. A second canoe-load of fine Kaua'i hogs arrived from the bountiful Queen Ka-maka-helei.

Finally, on March 15, a month after their Commander's death at Kealakekua Bay, Clerke turned the ships north. Gloom fell over the men at the remembrance of their Captain's loss and at the prospect of once again facing the rigors of the icy Arctic seas. As the lovely islands receded into the distance, Captain Clerke read them the Articles of War.

The Kamchatka Peninsula was sighted on April 23 and, at the harbor of St. Peter and Paul (Petropavlovsk), they were cordially received by the Russians. Clerke asked them to deliver a letter to England by the long overland route. This letter actually reached the Admiralty with the news of the disaster at Kealakekua Bay eight months before the voyage ended.

Captain Clerke pushed the ships through dense fog and thick ice floes in one last attempt to find a northwest passage. Further attempts were hopeless, and conscious of his own approaching death, he turned back fifteen miles from the point which Cook had reached the year before.

Only a few weeks later, in August 1779, the brave Clerke died and was buried at Petropavlovsk. John Gore took command of the *Resolution* and James King took over the *Discovery*. Gore headed for the Japanese coast hoping to survey as much of it as possible, but gale winds split the worn-out sails and snapped the rotten cordage.

The European settlement of Macao was reached on December 1, 1779. Here, the crews turned a handsome profit trading the furs they had on board to the Chinese who eagerly bought them. This was a portent, for the fur trade between North America and China would soon become important.

Though the war of England with the American colonies was in progress, French and American ships had been ordered not to molest the Cook expedition. The long voyage home took most of the year 1780. Gore brought the ships via the Cape of Good Hope into the Atlantic at last and, on October 6, 1780, came to anchor at Deptford. The voyage had lasted four years, two months, and twenty-two days.

COOK'S ACHIEVEMENT

During that long voyage, the *Resolution* had lost only four men from illness; three of them, Clerke included, had been in poor health when the voyage began. The *Discovery* returned with her crew intact… Cook had shown that scurvy need not be a major problem on long voyages.

In eleven years of geographical discovery, Cook had proved that the Pacific was more vast and varied than most geographers had imagined. He had shown that the unknown southern continent, if it existed, lay too far to the south to support life. He proved that there was no practicable northern passage through which ships of trade might sail.

Professor J. C. Beaglehole, who spent a lifetime studying Cook's life and voyages, had this to say about the character of his leadership: "The humanity that is kindness, understanding, tolerance, and wisdom in the treatment of men, a quality practiced naturally as well as planned for, is what gave Cook's voyages their success, as much as the soundness of his seamanship and the brilliance of his navigation."

His legacy was knowledge; his monument is the map of the Pacific.

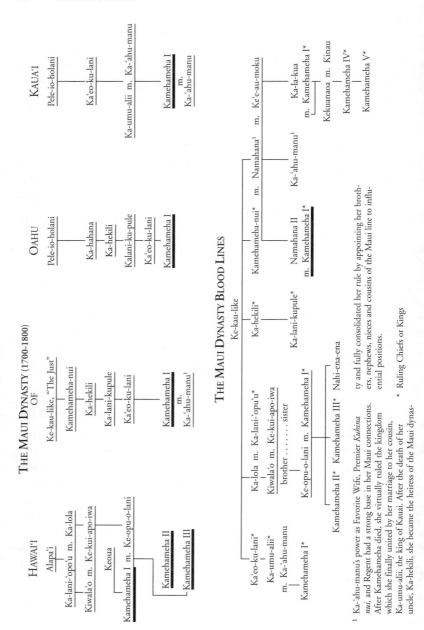

THE MAUI DYNASTY (1700-1800) OF

HAWAI'I

OAHU

KAUA'I

THE MAUI DYNASTY BLOOD LINES

[1] Ka-'ahu-manu's power as Favorite Wife, Premier *Kuhina nui*, and Regent had a strong base in her Maui connections. After Kamehameha died, she virtually ruled the kingdom which she finally united by her marriage to her cousin, Ka-umu-alii, the king of Kauai. After the death of her uncle, Ka-hekili, she became the heiress of the Maui dynasty and fully consolidated her rule by appointing her brothers, nephews, nieces and cousins of the Maui line to influential positions.

* Ruling Chiefs or Kings

CHAPTER 4

THE FINAL BATTLES: 1780-1794

Cook gave the chiefs their first sight of weapons that might transform war and turn an enterprising ali'i into a king.

— Gavan Daws, *Shoal of Time*

As contacts increased, the demand for weapons by the chiefs became insistent. They did not have to wait long to get them. Cook's discoveries had led to the opening of a new trade in furs with the northwest coast of America. Ships plying between there and China began to stop at the Islands for rendezvous and refreshment between voyages.

The intense bargaining for guns began, often accompanied by violence on both sides. "Many of the Hawaiians were marked with venereal sores, and they made it clear that their delight in owning a gun would be doubled if they could get one by killing a white man," and some of the white traders saw nothing wrong in arming one Hawaiian chief against another. Sometimes guns were sold to several factions who were then encouraged to shoot each other. Others sold defective gunpowder or guns that took their toll in injuries or deaths. The majority of the captains, however, traded fairly with the Hawaiians, maintaining friendly and mutually profitable relations.

Nevertheless, the demand for guns became more intense, and ships came in increasing numbers. For several seasons on the west coast of Hawai'i, the chiefs refused to sell hogs unless they were paid for in arms. A good example of the demand is found in the journals of Captain George Vancouver, the English captain who became Kamehameha's friend and advisor. Vancouver refused to sell arms to the chiefs, to their great disappointment. Yet, he did help Kamehameha to build a more formidable weapon of war than guns or cannon: a ship; the first ship to be built in Hawai'i. She was christened the *Britannia* and took part in the last phases of the war.

As possession of guns and iron weapons increased, the whole nature of Hawaiian warfare changed. The relations between the Hawaiians and the haoles changed at the same time. Sometimes anchors and boats were stolen with the idea that they could be ransomed for guns and ammunition or kept so that their iron could be turned into hand weapons and tools.

Cables were cut, copper removed from ships' bottoms, and boats disappeared in the night. When the haole captains complained, the chiefs were blamed, and they, in turn, blamed one another. "Ka-hekili was a master of ambiguity, and on Hawai'i, Kamehameha and the dashing chief, Kaiana, raised evasion and contradiction to a high art."

The traffic in arms continued to grow, and between 1785 and 1794 it is estimated that as many as thirty-five English ships and "at least fifteen American ships called at Hawai'i...yet, despite the violence, most ships were able to fill their water casks and salt down their hogs without trouble."

THE OLOWALU MASSACRE

Into these troubled waters an American ship named the *Eleanora* appeared in 1790. She was a merchantman in the fur trade commanded by Captain Simon Metcalf. At the end of January she anchored off Honua'ula, the village observed four years earlier by La Pérouse on his visit to Maui. While bartering there for provisions, the ship's boat, tied astern, was stolen during the night, and the sailor guarding the boat was slain. The boat was taken ashore and burned for its fittings of iron.

This incident resulted in the cruel massacre at Olowalu, Maui, which had indirect but important effects on the wars of the chiefs. Many descriptions of the massacre exist, one of the contemporary accounts having been published in the *Columbian Sentinel*, a newspaper of Boston in 1791. John Young, boatswain of the *Eleanora*, gave a full account to Vancouver, which he published in his *Journal*. Still another account is found in the logbook of the whale ship *Massachusetts*, now in the Library of the Peabody Museum of Salem.

When Metcalf discovered the loss of his boat and his crewman, he was in an evil mood. He turned out all the women aboard the *Eleanora* and then fired on a trading canoe, killing or wounding several Hawaiians. A man was caught swimming underneath the ship. Metcalf wanted to hang this man but gave in to the strong objections of his officers. Instead, he bombarded the villages with grapeshot, then sent men to set fire to the huts and the heiau.

Metcalf then sailed along the shore toward the village of Olowalu suspecting that the men who had brought hogs from there were responsible for the theft of the boat and the murder of the watchman. Next morning the High Chiefess Ka-lola* declared a tabu restricting canoes from approaching the *Eleanora*. Those who disobeyed were threatened with death by burning. Ka-lola alone among Hawaiian chiefs possessed this power, called the "burning kapu" or *mau'umae*, meaning "withered grass." The tabu lasted three days, but on the fourth day canoes went forth in great numbers to trade with the foreigners, now anchored off Olowalu.

The chief Ka-'opu-iki, husband of Ka-lola, came aboard offering to return the boat and the missing sailor. Metcalf promised a rich reward for their return. The chief returned bringing only a piece of the boat's keel and a pair of stripped thighbones, claiming the reward.

The officers, now incensed themselves, suggested hanging a few chiefs from the yardarm, but Metcalf prepared a more terrible revenge. Be it said that his officers did try to dissuade him, but he then encouraged the trading canoes to come out to the *Eleanora*, and, when a large number had gathered, he shunted them, all unsuspecting, to the ship's starboard side.

Ordering his gundeck ports opened and the swivel and brass guns on deck manned, he gave the order to fire.

"Within minutes, the sea was red with blood...Metcalf weighed anchor and sailed for the island of Hawaii, leaving the natives to drag for their dead with fishhooks." At least a hundred innocent natives were killed and more than a hundred wounded. Dozens of bodies were never found.

---

* This was the same chiefess, sister of Ka-hekili, who had been "sacred wife" to King Ka-lani-'opu'u before his death. At the time of the massacre, she was living at Olowalu with her second husband, the chief Ka-'opu-iki.

"The dead were heaped on the sands at Olowalu...The battle was called Kalolopahu, 'the spilled brains.' Wives, children, parents, and friends came to mourn over their dead; and the sound of loud wailing arose."

The *Eleanora* sailed away to Hawai'i seeking a rendezvous with another ship belonging to Metcalf. This was the *Fair American*, a small sloop commanded by Metcalf's son, Thomas. The Fair American had become separated from the *Eleanora* on the northwest coast of America and at the time of the massacre on Maui was searching for the elder Metcalf's ship along the western coast of Hawai'i.

The High Chief, Ka-me'e-ia-moku, ally of Kamehameha, seeing the *Fair American* cruising the coast near his district, decided to kill the crew and capture the ship. This powerful chief had been insulted by Simon Metcalf on an earlier occasion when he was struck with a rope as he sought to board the *Eleanora*. Ka-me'e-ia-moku swore revenge upon the next ship that appeared and, seeing a chance to secure a fine vessel with all its equipment, boarded the sloop with his men, who killed four of the crew, including young Metcalf.

One man, Isaac Davis, escaped with his life when a more merciful chief intervened. Davis was taken ashore to be held prisoner of Kamehameha. At the same time, the *Eleanora* put in at Kealakekua Bay where Metcalf allowed one man to go ashore. This man was the Englishman John Young whom Kamehameha also held against his will, fearing that if Young returned to the *Eleanora*, Metcalf would learn of the fate of his son and the *Fair American* and take revenge on the Hawaiians. Metcalf never found out what happened and was killed, along with another son, some years later by Indians on the northwest American coast.

Young and Davis became the companions and advisers (and gunners) to Kamehameha. The *Fair American* was a welcome addition to Kamehameha's war machine. She was stripped of her guns, including a small cannon which was christened Lopaka, an Hawaiian version of the name Robert. The sloop was then completely refitted and played an important part in subsequent battles.

Isaac Davis and John Young tried unsuccessfully to escape but eventually became reconciled to their fate and settled with

Hawaiian wives on lands granted by the King in their adopted country. The granddaughter of John Young became the Hawaiian Queen Emma, wife of Kamehameha IV.

WAR OF THE HAWAIIAN SUCCESSION

After the dramatic advent and departure of the Cook expedition and the end of the Makahiki season, there was a brief lull. Then the wars of the ruling chiefs were resumed. Ka-lani-'opu'u, who had spent a lifetime at war against Maui, never quite conquering the island, spent his last years drinking kawa and enjoying his favorite entertainment, the hula dancing in which the old King himself would often join. Ka-lani-'opu'u died in 1781 or 1782. Before his death, he had designated his highborn son, Kiwala'o, as his heir. At the same time, he designated his nephew, Kamehameha, as guardian of the war god, Ku-'ka'ili-moku.

Ka-hekili, on Maui, hearing of his opponent's death and the struggle for power which ensued between Kamehameha and the sons of Ka-lani-'opu'u, chose this moment to renew the war. Determined to rid Maui of Hawai'i's oppression, he set out to reconquer Hana and reunite Maui's eastern end with the Maui kingdom.

The chiefs of Hana, grandsons of the great Hawaiian chief Keawe and related to other chiefs of the Big Island, were loyal to Hawai'i. Hearing of Ka-hekili's preparations, they readied themselves for battle.

Ka-hekili divided his forces. One group was marched through the crater of Haleakala by the ancient trail and down the Kaupo gap. The rest of his forces the King sent out of the crater by the Ko'olau Gap. He planned to make a pincers movement on Hana and the fortress rock of Ka'uiki.

As the war dragged on, the defenders were able to hold out against the Maui forces for an entire year. At last, Ka-hekili, learning of the secret sources of water which sustained the besieged fortress, cut off the supply, and the defenders, dying of thirst, were finished off by Ka-hekili's warriors. A few of the chiefs tried to escape by lowering canoes from the steep sides of Ka'uiki. Two of the Hana chiefs escaped, but all the rest—chiefs, warriors, and commoners—were slain. The Hawaiian historian Kamakau, wrote: "Those who were eye-witnesses say there never was a more dreadful slaughter than in this war. At the heiaus below Ka'uiki were numerous ovens where the corpses were burned and left to dry in the sun."

In 1782, Ka-hekili, once again ruler in his own island kingdom, retired to cultivate his fertile fields and care for his people.

But Ka-hekili's cultivation of the land was short-lived. It must have been but a respite and preparation for the continuation of his unceasing fight to free Maui from the oppression of the Hawaiian chiefs and to conquer the Big Island. Now he turned against Kamehameha, sending some of his best fighters across the channel to aid his enemies in the struggle for control of the Big Island kingdom. In the fighting, the warriors of Ka-hekili wounded or killed a number of Kamehameha's best men before withdrawing to Maui, thus winning nothing but the enmity of that chief.

KA-HEKILI CONQUERS O'AHU

Ka-hekili, unsuccessful in his thrust against Kamehameha, now turned his attention toward O'ahu. The ruling chief of O'ahu was Ka-hekili's nephew and foster son, the ally who had sent reinforcements to Ka-hekili when Ka-lani-'opu'u was still on Maui warring against him.

Ka-hekili pretended to support the alliance with the ruling chief, Ka-hahana, but secretly prepared for war. He waited several years, biding his time. Ka-hahana became careless and mistakenly trusted the intentions of his foster father on Maui.

The O'ahu chief was living in Nu'uanu Valley above Honolulu when he received the news that Ka-hekili had landed on the beaches with a large fleet of war canoes and was gathering his warriors about him for an attack on the defenders of O'ahu.

In January 1783, a decisive battle was fought. Ka-hekili's wife, Kau-wahine, who was also a noted fighter, took part in this battle. "The waters of the stream of Kahe-iki ran red with blood from the heaps of broken corpses that fell into the water." Confusion seized the ranks; the warriors of Ka-hahana were dispersed while he and his wife fled to the forest. Thus, Oʻahu and Molokaʻi were taken by Ka-hekili. The Oʻahu chief and his wife lived secretly on Oʻahu for two and a half years, protected and supported by the people. When they were found, Ka-hekili had them put to death.

But this did not end the carnage. A plot to kill Ka-hekili, who was living at Kailua on Oʻahu, was discovered to have been organized by the chief of the ʻEwa district. Ka-hekili sent his troops in and attacked the districts of Kona and ʻEwa, where "men, women and children were massacred. All the Oʻahu chiefs were killed and the chiefesses tortured."*

Ka-hekili now controlled Oʻahu, but peace was not to be his. Fighting erupted on his home island of Maui among minor chiefs. At the same time, he learned of the growing threat from Hawaiʻi, where Kamehameha had defeated all rivals except the aliʻi Keoua and had gained control of most of the island kingdom. Ka-hekili's son and designated heir, Ka-lani-ku-pule, was dispatched to Wailuku to prepare for the coming attack. Ka-lani-ku-pule took with him Maui's war leaders and Ka-hekili's best warriors, the battle-scarred veterans of the war on Oʻahu.

KAMEHAMEHA CONQUERS MAUI, 1790

The epic struggle between the forces of Ka-hekili and Kamehameha for hegemony of the islands reached a climax in the battle of Kepaniwai ("The damming of the waters") in Maui's ʻIao Valley in 1790. Kamehameha was the victor in this bloody fight, the first major battle in which the superiority of western armaments and military tactics played the decisive role. It was by no means the last battle, but it was a decisive defeat for the Maui

---

* Kamakau described Ka-hekili as especially cruel to his enemies. This is to be doubted as it was customary, even expected in the old style battles of the aliʻi chiefs, that the losers in battle would lose their lives. Ka-hekili was probably no more nor less cruel than the other warring chiefs.

king, and it effectively removed the Maui kingdom from the path of the conqueror.

In nine years of bloody struggle, Kamehameha had emerged as the most feared and powerful of the warring chiefs in the Islands. As a young warrior, he had first seen the ships, met the first haoles, and had begun to note carefully the sources of their power when Cook's ships lay off Maui in 1778. He was present at Kealakekua Bay during the Cook sojourn there and was often a visitor to the ships where, on one occasion, Nathaniel Portlock, armorer on board H.M.S. *Discovery*, observed Kamehameha trading Captain Clerke a feather cloak for nine iron daggers. Some of the British officers thought they saw him at the death of Cook and were told he was wounded in the bombardment. He was also reported to have possession of Cook's hair, which added to his already powerful mana as a fighter chief.

Kamehameha had defeated his three major rivals one by one. Kiwalaʻo (the heir) was slain at the important battle of Mokuohai. The younger heir, Keoua, had defeated and killed the brother of Ka-lani-ʻopuʻu who controlled the Hilo districts of the island. The struggle for power had narrowed to the cousins, Kamehameha and Keoua. In another battle in 1782, Kamehameha had established himself as the strongest contestant for power on Hawaiʻi without, however, winning a decisive victory.

Four more years of campaigning followed without a final settlement among the contesting chiefs, and in 1786 the threat to the usurper's bid for power came from the direction of Maui.

Ka-hekili, an aliʻi of the older generation of warrior chiefs, had always been strong enough to resist invasion from Hawaiʻi, but by 1786 he had become the most powerful king in the Islands. He now controlled Maui, Molokaʻi, and Lanaʻi and had made himself the conqueror of Oʻahu, perhaps the richest prize of all.

In addition, Ka-hekili had a working agreement with his brother, Ka-ʻeo-ku-lani, the ruler of Kauaʻi. By 1790, Ka-hekili had become the greatest threat to Kamehameha's bid for power.

Kamehameha now decided to take the war from Hawaiʻi to Maui and thus convert the internal struggle on Hawaiʻi to a war for higher stakes; i.e., control of all the islands and the establishment of an island kingdom. If he could defeat the powerful ruler of all the islands beyond Hawai'i, he could rule supreme.

Kamehameha brought all his forces to the invasion of Maui. He took with him his feather war god, Ku-'ka'ili-moku, the basket-work head with staring shell eyes and the wide grin embellished with dogs' teeth. The feathers "bristled and stood up straight, a good omen."

Kamehameha won the first battle and then, with his full war machine, advanced along the north shore in a huge fleet of canoes. With him were Lopaka the cannon, swivel guns mounted on canoes, and Young and Davis to navigate the *Fair American* and to deploy and fire the artillery. He landed at Kahului where the ali'i prince, the son of Ka-hekili, was awaiting the attack.

The Maui defenders retreated into the steep 'Iao Valley. While women and children and old men watched from the hills, Isaac Davis and John Young cannonaded the Maui army into flight. Ka-lani-ku-pule, with most of the Maui chiefs, escaped through the mountains to Olowalu and then Lahaina whence he brought the bad news to his father on O'ahu.

Accompanying the prince and the Maui chiefs in their flight were the dowager queen of Hawai'i, Ka-lola, and her granddaughter, whose father had been slain by Kamehameha. This granddaughter, then about eleven, was the sacred and tabu chiefess, Ke-opu-o-lani. The child was carried on the shoulders of her kahu (guardian) to Lahaina and from there to Moloka'i, where Ka-lola and her retinue camped as the queen was too ill to travel further.

Kamehameha sent messengers to Ka-lola on Moloka'i and beyond to Ka-hekili on O'ahu. The message to Ka-lola was the offer of protection of her family and especially of the tabu chief-ess, Ke-opu-o-lani. He then sailed for Moloka'i. Ka-lola, near death, gave the sacred child to Kamehameha.

The message to Ka-hekili was in the form of two stones: one black, the other white. Ka-hekili read the challenge correctly. The white stone meant peace; the black meant war. Ka-hekili told the messengers: "Go back and tell Kamehameha to return to Hawai'i and when the black kapa covers Ka-hekili and the black pig rests at his nose, then is the time to cast stones." (The interpretation: "When I die, the kingdom will be yours.") Ka-hekili had no intention of yielding to Kamehameha's pressures and set about at once to put his affairs in order.

Kamehameha was still on Moloka'i with all his fleet and land forces when word came of rebellion on Hawai'i. He returned at once and resumed his war against Keoua, the second son of old Ka-lani-'opu'u, who foolishly had killed his uncle, the chief at Hilo, and was now ravaging the lands of Kamehameha, burning villages and killing his people.

The cousins fought and fought again without decisive victory for either side. Keoua and his army then suffered a setback that was taken as an augury of the disfavor of the gods, especially Pele, the goddess of the volcanoes.

Keoua, after a fierce battle with Kamehameha, had decided to withdraw with his warriors, his retinue, and their families by a path close to the crater of Kilauea. As they passed, an eruption threw a cloud of hot smoke across the sun, hot cinders fell on bare bodies.

Those in the rear of the marching line rushed ahead to find a horrifying sight. Reaching their comrades in the vanguard, "they discovered them all to have become corpses. Some were lying down, and others were sitting upright clasping with dying grasp their wives and children, and joining noses (their form of expressing affection) as in the act of taking a final leave."

In the complicated nine-year struggle for power, this was a blow to Keoua's side, more psychological than material, as both contestants still seemed evenly matched.

Then, Kamehameha began building the great war heiau on the hill called Pu'u-kohola ("Hill of the Whale") overlooking Kawaihae Bay. It was dedicated to his war god, Ku-'ka'ili-moku, and from the first was intended for the offering of human sacrifice. "Psychological warfare might succeed where force of arms could not prevail."

Every step of the designing and building was accompanied by special prayers, rituals, and sacrifices. The chiefs themselves were put to work carrying rocks, and thousands of commoners took part in the construction. The "Hill of the Whale" itself carried great mana as its lower slope was the site of the ancient Mailekini Heiau.

This act of temple building may have spurred the chiefs of the other islands to make an attack before it was too late. A great fleet was collected which carried the combined forces of Oʻahu, Maui, Molokaʻi, and Kauaʻi to Waimana Bay near the Waipio Valley off Hawaiʻi's Hamakua coast.

Kamehameha interrupted his temple building to meet the enemy fleet off Waipio. A bloody sea battle ensued, the Battle of the Red-Mouthed Gun (Ke-pa-waha-ula-ula), so called because both sides used guns and cannon.* But Kamehameha once more held the advantage in arms, and his little sloop, the *Fair American,* mounted with two cannon, added to the awful slaughter. The battle was not a clear victory for either side, but it was the end of the power of the invaders who returned to prepare for the coming invasion of their own islands.

The temple was built. For its final dedication the sacrifice of a tabu or very high chief was required. Kamehameha had invited his arch rival, Keoua, to the dedication. Surprisingly, Keoua came willingly, though against the advice of his chiefs and priests. He seemed to have lost all will to continue the struggle. His close companions who accompanied him in his canoe also seem to have been resigned to join him in death.

As the young prince landed at the bay of Kawaihae, resplendent in the most ancient and royal of feather cloaks, Keoua was speared by Kamehameha's father-in-law and top war chief, Keʻe-au-moku; twenty-four of his attendants were also slain, and the body of Keoua was carried to Puʻu-kohola and placed in sacrifice on the altar of the war heiau of Kamehameha. Keoua's retainers mourned him: "The rain drives down from the cliffs above, the tears for my chief drop down on the heads of the people."

Kamehameha was now lord of Hawaiʻi, having repulsed Ka-hekili's combined war fleet and eliminated his remaining rival on Hawaiʻi. Ka-hekili returned to Oʻahu with his half brother and

---

* Ka-hekili brought to this battle his gunner, his war dogs, and his special group of fighting men called the *Pahupas.* They were tattooed black on one side, like the King. Portlock saw some of these fierce-looking warriors when he visited at Waimea Bay (Oʻahu) in 1794.

closest ally, Ka-'eo-ku-lani, chief of Kaua'i, to nurse his wounds and prepare for the final showdown. During the interval, he did return to Maui for a time where he occasionally exchanged gifts with haole ship captains.

The forces of Ka-hekili and Kamehameha never met again. The old chief and King, said to be eighty-seven, died in 1794 on O'ahu. His body was treated in the ancient way at the sacred heiau at Le'ahi (Diamond Head) and was claimed by his half brothers, the twin guardians of Kamehameha,* who are supposed to have buried his bones secretly in a cave, "perhaps at Kaloko in north Kohala" on Hawai'i; perhaps on Moloka'i.

Another war of succession between his heirs soon broke out in open battles, and the empire of the dynasty of Ke-kau-like, the great Maui progenitor, began to fall apart. Maui, Moloka'i, and Lana'i could not resist the conqueror and were reconquered by 1794. O'ahu fell in 1795. By 1810, Kaua'i agreed to Kamehameha's overlordship of that island and his rule of all Hawai'i was undisputed.

One more revolt led Kamehameha back to Hawai'i where he defeated and sacrificed the rebellious chief, then settled back on his home grounds for the next six years. These were years of peace and consolidation during which Kamehameha proved to be as wise an administrator as he had been a bold and successful war lord.

With the help of Ka-'ahu-manu, granddaughter of Ke-kau-like, who became queen, and her brothers and sisters of the Maui dynasty of Ke-kau-like, Kamehameha established a royal line which lasted for a hundred years.

---

* It is an odd fact, yet one confirmed by all the earlier historians, that the guardians of Kamehameha from the time of his birth until their deaths, were the twin sons of Ke-kau-like of Maui and thus the half brothers of Kamehameha's arch enemy, Ka-hekili. These two chiefs remained, through their lives, faithful to Kamehameha and were fully trusted by him. It is believed that these Maui chiefs were sent by their brother, Ka-hekili to protect Kamehameha at the Hawaiian court because he believed that Kamehameha was his own natural son. If this is the case, it would explain why the kahu(s) of the conqueror were allowed to claim the body of Ka-hekili from his own sons and take it to the island of Hawai'i for burial. The figures standing on either side of the royal coat of arms of Hawai'i represent these faithful guardians.

CHAPTER 5

FRENCH AND BRITISH ON MAUI: 1786-1796

THE FRENCH LANDING

Although Cook is credited with being the first westerner to see Maui, he did not attempt to land there. The first explorer from Europe to do so was a Frenchman, Admiral Jean François Galaup, Compte de la Pérouse. Considered second only to Cook, he was the foremost French explorer of the Pacific in the eighteenth century. "Although he spent but a brief time on Maui, the observations La Pérouse consigned to his journal constitute a firsthand document indispensable for the study of the early history of the island."

In March 1786, La Pérouse sailed from Concepción in Chile and visited Easter Island where he found the natives friendly and checked out the observations of Cook. Here, a bold native relieved the Admiral of his finest chapeau. From Easter Island he sailed for Hawai'i.

In an interesting note from his journal he wrote: "The men began to catch tuna, which followed the frigates all the way to the Sandwich Islands and provided complete ration for the crews almost every day for a month and a half. This excellent nourishment kept them in the best of health." They were now sailing in unknown seas, following a route parallel to that taken by Captain Cook in 1777.

After seeing various signs that land was near, on May 28, 1786, La Pérouse sighted the snow-capped mountains of Hawai'i and, soon afterwards, "the peaks of Maui, not quite so high…" He spent the night tacking, awaiting daybreak to enter the channel between these two islands and to find an anchorage to the leeward of Maui.

It was seven and a half years after Cook's discovery, but *Astrolabe* and *Boussole* were not the first ships to reach Hawai'i after Cook. The English ships *King George* and *Queen Charlotte*, under command of Captains Nathaniel Portlock and George Dixon, had sighted Hawai'i just four days ahead of the Frenchmen. The English captains, both veterans of Cook's Third Voyage, lingered only two days at Kealakekua, when they weighed anchor to cruise around Maui, Lana'i, and Moloka'i. Thus, they must have been in the same waters though they neither met nor became aware of each other's presence. It is possible that the French and English ships passed within viewing distance during the night.

From the description in his log, it appears that La Pérouse must have entered the Alenuihaha Channel near Hana, for they sighted the western tip of Maui in the distance, then, seeking an anchorage near Molokini, turned south to run along the eastern end–past Hamoa, the lush valleys at Kipahulu and in sight of Kaupo, then the most populous part of East Maui.

La Pérouse wrote vividly in his journal: "At nine in the morning the point of Mowee bore west 15° north… The aspect of the island was delightful, I coasted along its shore at the distance of a league…We beheld water falling in cascades from the mountains and running in streams to the sea after having watered the habitations of the natives, which are so numerous that a space of three or four leagues may be taken for a single village. But all the huts are on the seacoast, and the mountains are so near that the habitable part of the island appeared to be less than half a league in depth.

"To get an idea of what we felt, one has to be a seaman and be reduced, as we were, in a burning climate, to a single bottle of water a day. The trees which crowned the mountains and the verdure of the banana plants that surrounded the habitations produced inexpressible charms to our senses, but the sea beat upon the coast with the utmost violence and kept us in the situation of Tantalus, desiring and devouring with our eyes what was impossible for us to attain."

La Pérouse had decided that a safe anchorage would be found at the islet called Molokini and was determined to reach the haven before nightfall. Hence, he did not shorten sail when the Hawaiians appeared in canoes ready for trade. About 150 canoes swarmed toward the French ships eager to trade their hogs and fruits for pieces of iron.

"Almost all these canoes boarded one or the other of the frigates. But our rate of speed was so great that they filled with water, and the islanders were obliged to let go the rope which we had thrown out to them and swim away. They first hastened after their hogs, which they brought back in their arms, lifted them on their shoulders into their boats, out of which they emptied the water, and cheerfully entering them again, endeavoring by utmost efforts to recover the position they had lost near our frigates, and which had been instantly occupied by others who also met with the same accident. Of these canoes, at least forty were upset and, though the trading between us and these honest Indians was infinitely agreeable to both parties, it was impossible for us to procure more than fifteen hogs and some fruits and we lost the opportunity of bargaining for more than three hundred others."

La Pérouse then describes the canoes as twenty-four-foot outriggers each containing about five men. He had one of them weighed and found it weighed only fifty pounds, remarking on his surprise at the discovery that the islanders can travel up to sixty leagues in them, even in high seas.

He continues his description of the land as seen from the flagship *Boussole*. After passing the fertile valley of Kaupo, the mountains seemed to him to recede into the interior; no more waterfalls were seen; there were fewer trees, and the villages were fewer and further separated. No anchorage was found here, to his disappointment. Moving swiftly along the dry lee shore, he saw the marks of a large lava flow cascading down the sides of the mountain and into the sea.

The *Astrolabe* had already dropped anchor in the shallow bay which was surrounded by black lava rocks. La Pérouse brought the *Boussole* in to within a mile of shore where he anchored in the shelter of a large promontory. The name of La Pérouse Bay perpetuates the memory of his visit.

The anchorage was not secure, and puffs of wind from over the mountain occasioned squalls that caused the ships to drag anchor continually. As the ships were warped in closer to the shore, several small villages were observed. The ship's artist on the *Astrolabe* produced a drawing which shows the Frenchmen at anchor. It is an accurate rendering of the scene exactly as it is today except that the villages are now deserted ruins. One can even find the wells, canoe sheds and low, rock walls which were originally foundations for the grass houses that La Pérouse saw. Thus, the journal of the French Admiral contains the first detailed description by visitors to the land. Although Captain Clerke attempted to chart this side of Maui after Cook's death in February 1779, the ships had been swept along by strong currents, and a landing had not been attempted.

Canoes came out immediately to the ships to barter their hogs and vegetables for iron. La Pérouse would not allow them to come aboard saying that he was taboo (kapu). The Hawaiians understood this very well. However, he wrote: "M. de Langle [the captain of the *Astrolabe*], who had not taken the same precaution, had his decks crowded in an instant with a multitude of Indians. But they were so docile and so apprehensive of giving offence that it was extremely easy to prevail upon them to return to their boats."

The French captain surmised that this method of trading and knowledge of iron came not from the English, but were new proofs that islanders had earlier had communications with the Spanish. He buttressed this idea with the theory that the Spanish did not make known their discovery because they wished to keep it from pirates who infested the western seas of America, and who might find provisions and a haven there. La Pérouse spent a calm night at anchor, and early in the morning of May 30, 1786, set off to make his landing on Maui. La Pérouse reported in his journal:

> At eight in the morning four boats belonging to the two frigates were ready to set off. The first carried twenty armed soldiers, commanded by Pierrevert, one of the lieutenants. M. de Langle and myself with all the gentlemen and officers who were not detained by their duty on board, were in the two others. This preparation did not alarm the natives who since daybreak had been alongside

in their canoes…About a hundred and twenty persons, men and women, waited for us on the shore . . . the women showed by the most expressive gestures that there was no mark of kindness they were not disposed to confer upon us, and the men in the most respectful attitude endeavored to discover the motive of our visit in order to anticipate our desires…I had no idea of a people so mild and attentive.

The journal of Dr. Rollin, the doctor aboard the Boussole, describes the common people whom they met on Maui's south shore. He found them amply provided with all the necessities of life but not as healthy as the Easter Islanders:

> Their average height is about 5 feet 3 inches; they are somewhat less fleshy, and they have coarse features, thick eyebrows, black eyes which without being hard express self-confidence, prominent cheek-bones, slightly widened nostrils, thick lips, a large mouth, and teeth which are somewhat wide but quite fine and straight. Their hair is black and cut in the pattern of a helmet. Worn very long, like the flowing crest of a helmet, their hair is a reddish brown color at the ends…These people paint and tatoo their skin. They pierce their ears and nasal septa, and adorn themselves with rings inserted in these parts.
>
> The inhabitants in general however are mild and engaging in their behavior, and even show toward strangers a degree of politeness…The dress of both sexes consists of a sort of apron covering what nature bids them conceal, and another piece of similar cloth wrapped around the body.

Dr. Rollin's report discussed the signs of venereal disease he observed among the people. He had examined many lepers in the hospitals at Madeira and Manila and also observed the victims of elephantiasis in the South Seas.

Rollin, discussing the question of the introduction of the venereal by Captain Cook's crews, was inclined to believe that the disease existed in the islands before Cook. He thought that it probably was indigenous "or else had been introduced by former navigators."

This detailed description by the learned French doctor is typical of the approach of the experts on board the *Astrolabe* and *Boussole* who were following the example of the scientists of the Cook expeditions. They had been brought up in the encyclopedic atmosphere of the French Enlightenment and their orders contained instructions to observe, measure, and describe everything of interest which they might find in their travels.

THE FATE OF LA PÉROUSE

The French frigates set their course for the northwest coast of America where the first of a series of tragedies took place. They had discovered and anchored in a bay which La Pérouse named Frenchmen's Harbor (Lituja Bay) on July, 13, 1786. Three boats set out to make soundings in the bay. The *Astrolabe's* longboat and another from the *Boussole* were swamped in a fierce tide rip in the inlet, and not one of the twenty-one men aboard survived, nor were bodies, or even wreckage, recovered. The anguish of the good Captain La Pérouse and the remaining officers and men can hardly be imagined. The search was abandoned after eighteen days. A cenotaph of wood was raised as a memorial and a bottle buried at its base containing the inscription:

TWENTY-ONE BRAVE SAILORS PERISHED AT THE
ENTRANCE TO THIS HARBOR: WHOSOEVER YOU
MAY BE, MINGLE YOUR TEARS WITH OURS.

A second misfortune was to plague the expedition before the year 1787 was ended. La Pérouse had sailed to the Samoan Islands in search of urgently needed fresh provisions. Arriving at a large, well populated, and very fertile island which he called Mauna (probably

Tutuila), the frigates came to anchor. Captain de Langle, believing the natives friendly, led sixty-one men in the longboats into a coral-filled cove entered only by a narrow, windy channel. They were in search of fresh water, and the natives along the shore offered pigs and fruits for exchange.

Soon the boats were surrounded by many canoes, and 1,500 islanders had crowded onto the narrow beach along the little creek, causing disorder and confusion. M. de Langle distributed gifts, which led to fighting among the natives. The longboats, ordered to retreat, were then savagely attacked by the mob; the close quarters rendered the guns, already wet, almost useless. Abandoning the longboats, the men sought to climb aboard the pinnaces, which were still afloat. The longboats were instantly ripped apart. The mob, yelling ferociously, rushed forward trying to cut off the French withdrawal. The pinnaces cleared the reef with their cargo of wounded. They came alongside, and La Pérouse heard the tragic news of the death of Captain de Langle, his closest companion and second in command, along with the naturalist, Lamanon, the master-at-arms, Talin, and several of the sailors.

La Pérouse, one of the most humane of eighteenth-century ship commanders, refused to allow his men to fire upon the peaceful natives who filled about a hundred canoes still surrounding the ships. He was dissuaded from sending out a party in retaliation after his lieutenant pointed out the dangers of the reef and the lack of a secure anchorage, together with the certainty of further massacre if the ships went on the reefs.

La Pérouse hung about for two days hoping to find some way of recovering the bodies of his comrades; then, with a heavy heart, sailed on. He called this place Massacre Bay.

The third and final tragedy was the wreck of both French vessels early in 1788 during a hurricane off Vanikoro in the Santa Cruz Islands. For forty years no trace could be found of the great French explorer of the Pacific. Then an English captain, Peter Dillon, solved the mystery at least of the wrecks, various parts of which were salvaged and returned to France. Apparently, there were survivors at Vanikoro but none ever reached home.

The tragedy ended all hope that extensive scientific findings could result from the well-planned, well-equipped expedition. Only La Pérouse's foresight in sending back his journals from Kamchatka and Botany Bay saved the endeavor from total loss.*

SHIPS THAT PASSED IN THE NIGHT: MAY 30-JUNE 1, 1786

On Saturday, May 27, 1786, the *King George* and *Queen Charlotte* of the English expedition to the northwest coast of America left Kealakekua Bay heading for Maui. The next day, they stood off Hawai'i still trading for provisions, and on the morning of May 29 set their course for Maui, then about nine leagues off and in plain sight. By eight o'clock on the morning of May 30, Maui was four leagues distant and the west end of Lana'i NNW two leagues away. The ships thus coasted the southern side of Maui but did not find anchorage there. Perhaps they were swept past Maui just as the ships of Cook were swept along in February 1779, and just as La Pérouse would be when he left the anchorage at La Pérouse Bay on May 30.

The entry in Nathaniel Portlock's log for Tuesday, May 30, reads as follows: "During the night [May 29] we had fresh gales and cloudy weather, which occasioned us to shorten sail and tack occasionally. Towards morning the weather moderated. At eight o'clock Mowee bore from North half East to East North East *distant four leagues* [author's italics], and the West end of Ranai [Lana'i] North North West, two leagues distant."

At that very moment, with Portlock and George Dixon but four leagues off Maui on the same side, La Pérouse was anchored with his two frigates and was visiting the villages on the southern shore. It seems incredible that the British failed to see the French frigate or vice versa. The best guess is that the *King George* and *Queen Charlotte* had already passed along that side during the night, although the log places them four leagues off Maui in

* Viscount de Lesseps traveled from Kamchatka with La Pérouse's earlier journal. He made the difficult trip overland from Petropavlovsk across Siberia and reached Paris. Forty years later, he was able to identify positively the relics of La Pérouse recovered from Vanikoro. Among these relics were a silver sword guard and spoon which he had left aboard the *Boussole* and a small millstone which the expedition used to grind grain.

the morning of May 30. The English ships might have been too far ahead of the French to see or be seen. La Pérouse reported that the Hawaiians had been out in their canoes, 120 of them, men, women and children, "since the crack of dawn." If the Hawaiians knew of the Portlock-Dixon tall ships, they gave no indication of this to La Pérouse.

Then to add to the coincidence, the French frigates took the same north route heading for the southwest point of the island of Moloka'i "which I coasted at the distance of three quarters of a league, and came into the open sea, like the English [meaning Cook's ships], through the channel which separates the island of Woahoo [O'ahu], from that of Morotai [Moloka'i]." Just before this, La Pérouse had stood to the westward, "passing at an equal distance from the northwest point of the island of Tahoorowa [Kaho'olawe] and the southwest point of the island of Ranai [Lana'i]."

While La Pérouse was coasting the southwest shore of Moloka'i, Portlock and Dixon also stood for Moloka'i and were only three leagues off the west end. Portlock lay to during the night, and in the morning found his ships had been driven eight or nine leagues to the southwest, "so that instead of fetching with the West point of Moloka'i, as I expected...I found we scarcely should be able to weather the East point of Woahoo, round which we knew there was anchorage." Portlock-Dixon thus were in the same channel traversed by La Pérouse as he sailed out of the islands on May 31 and June 1, 1786.

So far as is known, there is no record of the French and British sighting each other, nor notice taken of the coincidence of their being off Maui's southeastern coast at the same time. Had they met, another interesting dimension might have been added to the history of Maui.

VANCOUVER, FRIEND OF HAWAI'I

A bright young midshipman who sailed with Cook on the Third Voyage, George Vancouver, was present on board H.M.S.

Resolution when his captain was killed at Kealakekua Bay. During that first visit, Kamehameha spent many hours aboard the *Resolution*, where the two first met under friendly auspices.

Fourteen years later, in February 1793, Vancouver, now captain and leader of his own expedition for the British government, sailed into Kealakekua Bay. He quickly learned that Kamehameha was now the paramount chief and king of the Island of Hawai'i, and he welcomed Kamehameha aboard his flagship (also named the *Discovery*). "On his entering the cabin, I again recognized the identical *Tamaahmaah* I had known some years before, by the savage austerity and gloom that was now diffused over the countenance of that chief." Kamehameha was indeed furious as, at this point in his visit to Vancouver, the High Chief Kaiana appeared in the cabin offering gifts of hogs and presenting the captain with a fine feather helmet.

The Chief, Ke'e-au-moku, also present at this meeting, then objected that Vancouver had refused to accept *his* offer of twenty of the finest hogs because there was no room for them on the already crowded ship. Vancouver was embarrassed by the rivalry of the Hawaiian chiefs but wrote in his log, "I was, however, fully determined on the measures to be persued; to pay my principal court to *Tamaahmaah*, as the King of the whole island" and, despite the displeasure he had noted in the King's reaction to Kaiana, Vancouver was impressed with Kamehameha's "open, cheerful, and sensible mind, combined with great generosity and goodness of disposition."

In this first encounter, Vancouver had already exhibited some talent for tact and diplomacy, which he later exerted in an admirable but fruitless attempt to organize a pact of peace between the warring chiefs of Maui and Hawai'i. On another occasion, Vancouver was to act as representative of the British King in arranging an agreement with Kamehameha and the Hawaiian chiefs to "cede" the island of Hawai'i to Great Britain. Although this was never recognized by the British government and was probably not considered by Kamehameha as more than an informal protective alliance, it was an important link between the British and the Islands.

There were other notable actions of Vancouver, who appears to have found a very real friendship with the Hawaiian king. He brought the first cattle to the Islands and persuaded Kamehameha to place a *kapu* on them for ten years so that they multiplied and became an important asset in trade and in the economy of the Islands. He established a strong friendship for Britain among the chiefs, especially Kamehameha, which was to have lasting impact upon island history.

VANCOUVER VISITS MAUI, 1793

After his visit with Kamehameha, Vancouver moved over to Maui on March 10, 1793. Following the path which La Pérouse and Portlock and Dixon had taken in 1786, he cruised off the Kipahulu-Kaupo districts, describing them as having "a verdant and fertile appearance, and...seemingly in an advanced state of cultivation. From the number of villages and distinct houses, we were led to consider it as tolerably well inhabited."

Observing the radical change from verdant to arid as the ship moved westward, Vancouver rounded the south point at La Pérouse Bay where a chief came out in the first decent canoe he had seen off Maui that day.

By this chief, Vancouver sent a handsome present to *Titee-ree* (Ka-hekili), the king of Maui, to accompany a message of friendship.

Vancouver finally came to anchor in the roadstead of Raheina (Lahaina) after observing closely the character of Maui's terrain along the southwest coast and the condition of the people and the land.

As Portlock had discovered seven years earlier, the western shores of Maui were in a state of devastation due to the depredations of the wars between Kamehameha and his chiefs and Ka-hekili and his sons and warriors. Those few Hawaiians who did come out to trade were observed to travel in worn and inferior canoes and often had little in the way of hogs or fruits to barter with the ships.

Even in Lahaina, Vancouver found indications of dire poverty: "Mowee and its neighboring islands were reduced to great indi-

gence by the wars in which they had for many years been engaged."
Vancouver was warned to be alert to possible attack on Maui. He
had been told all the details of the Olowalu Massacre by John
Young, who was an eyewitness, and he also suspected Maui's
Ka-hekili in his position as High Chief of Oʻahu of complicity in
the murder of Captain Hergest and Mr. Gooch of Vancouver's supply ship *Daedalus,* which earlier had visited Waimea Bay on Oʻahu
in search of fresh water and provisions.

VANCOUVER ARGUES FOR PEACE

The significance of Vancouver's three visits to Hawaiʻi in the
years 1793-1794 lies in his close association with the Kings
Kamehameha, Ka-hekili, and the other high chiefs of Hawaiʻi,
Maui, Kauaʻi and Oʻahu.

Vancouver made repeated arguments to the chiefs for a peaceful settlement and offered to act as personal ambassador to bring
about negotiations between Maui and Hawaiʻi. He suggested that a
chief be sent to Hawaiʻi from Maui with full powers to negotiate a
settlement, but the Hawaiʻi chiefs said that they would consider a
chief from Maui as a spy and "would instantly put him to death."
Kamehameha was obviously not enthusiastic about a settlement,
yet Vancouver continued his efforts, approaching Ka-hekili and
Ka-ʻeo on Maui. At first the Maui chiefs tried to persuade
Vancouver to stay at Maui and take their side in the struggle, which
he refused to do.

They listened attentively to his arguments, but were willing to
send a chief to Hawaiʻi only if Vancouver himself would take him to
Kamehameha in his ship under safe conduct. Vancouver felt he could
not spare the time to do this and, after several days at Lahaina where
he and King Ka-hekili and Ka-ʻeo exchanged visits, sailed on to Oʻahu
and finally Kauaʻi, where he was also welcomed as a friend.

Vancouver contributed to the stabilization of relations between
the chiefs and the visiting captains. He felt real friendship for
Kamehameha, and, though Ka-hekili was then at the end of his life

and impoverished by war, he was treated with the same respect and generosity as Vancouver had extended to Kamehameha.

Moreover, Vancouver was sincere in his efforts at peacemaking. Even though he saw long range benefits for Europeans, and especially Englishmen who would follow, he also had altruistic motives in urging the chiefs to make a peaceful settlement and halt the tragic destruction which was hurting their own people most of all. Vancouver handled the punishment of the murderers of Captain Herqest and his men with skill and with justice appropriate at the time to both British and Hawaiian concepts. Although it is possible that one or more of the three Hawaiian men executed for the murders was innocent, Vancouver rightly insisted that the executions be performed at the orders of the Oʻahu chiefs themselves and not by his orders.

Throughout his time in the Islands, he literally "stuck to his guns" when the chiefs begged him to sell them arms. He even refused the requests of Kamehameha by saying that King George of England had put a taboo on firearms.

A monument to George Vancouver is found at Kihei on the eastern shore of Maui near where he first met King Ka-hekili. It was placed there by people from Vancouver, B.C. in 1968.

CHAPTER 6

WOMEN'S LIB–HAWAIIAN STYLE: 1819-1832

*The eating kapus were most irksome and humiliating to
women; at this time [1819] there were two female chiefs
who had a very powerful influence in the affairs of the
nation: Keopuolani, mother of Liholiho and the highest
ranking ali'i in the kingdom; and Kaahumanu, who
shared the government with Liholiho. After the death of
Kamehameha I, both of these powerful chiefesses favored
the overthrow of the old system.*

– Kuykendall, *The Hawaiian Kingdom*

With the death of Ka-hekili, his brother, Ka-'eo-ku-lani,
and his son, Ka-lani-ku-pule, the rule of Maui by high
chiefs of the Ke-kau-like dynasty came to an end.
But the blood of the Maui chiefs persisted. It was carried by
the Queen, Ke-opu-o-lani, and into the royal line of successors
by her sons, Liholiho (Kamehameha II) and Kau-i-ke-aouli
(Kamehameha III). This blood ran also in the veins of Ka-'ahu-
manu, whose mother, the High Chiefess Na-mahana, was a high-
ranking daughter of Ke-kau-like.

The bitter wars of the chiefs had at last come to an end, but a
new influence was at work that could greatly change the character of
Hawaiian life and manners. Haoles (foreigners) had already visited or
taken residence in the Islands in increasing numbers, bringing with
them their virtues and their vices; their technology and their diseases.

The conquest of the Islands was completed, and Kamehameha
proceeded to consolidate his power and practice the arts of peace.
His old advisor, John Young, was appointed to govern the Big
Island, and he sent one of his most faithful military leaders to govern
Maui. This was the High Chief, Ke'e-au-moku, his general and the
father of Queen Ka-'ahu-manu.

After the wars, the restoration of Maui, especially Lahaina, had begun. Vancouver and others had already surveyed the harbor and roadstead, and ships came to anchor there in increasing numbers after 1796. For a time, Lahaina became the capital of the kingdom, and Kamehameha had built there a brick "palace" furnished in the English style for his beloved Ka-'ahu-manu.

In 1808 a visitor, Archibald Campbell, described this brick building in his journal and then wrote: "Maccalum [an English resident] informed me that it [Maui] was very fertile; that provisions were abundant, and much cheaper than either Owhyhee or Wahoo." Maui had recovered from the terrible wars of the 1790s.

"THE FAVORITE WIFE"

> *Listen ye, therefore, to my commands. This is the voice of Ka-'ahu-manu!*
>
> Dowager Queen on the departure of
> Kamehameha II for England in 1823.

Kamehameha I took Ka-'ahu-manu to wife not only for her beauty but because of her powerful connections. From the time of her marriage, she wielded immense power through the chiefs of her blood, whose allegiance to her husband was guaranteed as long as she held the special position of power for which we have only the inadequate title, "Favorite Wife."

After her husband's death, this female chief of the Maui line ruled (but did not reign) for thirteen years, first as Premier, then as Regent. Her parents, her brothers and sisters, her nieces and nephews and adopted children were appointed to the key positions in the island kingdom and thus were the sources of her power.

The name of this queen came from her maternal uncle, Ka-hekili-nui-'ahu-manu, last king of an independent Maui Island kingdom. When she was born in the cave at Hana, her parents, though no longer loyal to Ka-hekili, strangely enough gave the baby girl the name Ka-ʻahu-manu ("The Feather Cloak") from the name of her royal relative.

HAWAIʻI UNDER KA-ʻAHU-MANU

Elizabeth Ka-ʻahu-manu was a queen who, if she had lived in a more powerful nation, would rank near the top of any list of great queens in history.

She was beautiful, she was imperious and intelligent; she became a capable ruler, perhaps the most powerful ruler of the Islands after her husband; she loved powerful and handsome chiefs, one of whom was her first husband, Kamehameha the Great, and another, the charming Ka-umu-aliʻi, hereditary chief-king of Kauaʻi, whom she married when she was widow and Regent of the Kingdom.

In marrying the King of Kauaʻi, Ka-ʻahu-manu finally achieved what Kamehameha never actually accomplished–she bound Kauaʻi fully into the Kingdom through dynastic marriage and consolidation of power. She did this by virtually kidnapping the Kauaʻi king, marrying him, and then his son and heir, as well. On his death, she appointed her brother to govern Kauaʻi.

The High Chiefess Ka-ʻau-manu was born on Maui in a small cave at the foot of the hill of Kaʻuiki about 1768, the only daughter of the High Chiefs, Keʻe-au-moku and Na-mahana.

The Hawaiian historian, S. M. Kamakau, apparently quoting a description of the young Chiefess at the time she attracted the attention of Kamehameha, wrote as follows:

"A handsome woman, six feet tall, straight and well-formed was Ka-ʻahu-manu, without blemish and comely. Her arms were like the inside of a banana stalk, her fingers tapering, her palms pliable like kukunene grass, graceful in repose, her cheeks long in shape and pink as the bud of a banana stem; her eyes like those of a dove or the moho bird; her nose narrow and straight, in admirable proportion to her cheeks; her arched eyebrows shaped to the breadth of her forehead; her hair dark, wavy, and fine, her skin very light."

Kamakau tells us also that Ka-'ahu-manu was prized above all others by the King."All her requests were granted. She was allowed to enter the meetings of the high council" and eventually took her father's place therein, after his death in 1804. Kamehameha also granted to her the power of pardon, while her lands were turned into places of refuge.

The death of her royal husband was both a tragedy and a triumph for the Favorite Wife. Undoubtedly, she loved the King, and she also enjoyed the extraordinary powers which he had conferred upon her. Iolani Liholiho was already designated the heir to the throne, but for a short time there was uncertainty about the transfer of power while the rituals surrounding the preparations for burial were carried out.

Even in the matter of the burial, Ka-'ahu-manu had a voice: at the council of the chiefs regarding disposition of the body, one and another offering to take it, Ka-'ahu-manu said "faintly," according to Kamakau, "This body is not ours; ours was the breath, the body belongs to one of the chiefs." Apparently, she meant Liholiho, who, with his mother, took the remains in a canoe to a secret cave where it was placed by Hoapili. "The morning star alone knows where Kamehameha's bones are guarded."

After the King's death, Ka-'ahu-manu claimed that Kamehameha had willed to her the unique position of *kuhina nui*, which placed her as prime minister and co-ruler with his son, Iolani Liholiho. The new King was proclaimed at the council of chiefs, the council agreeing that Ka-'ahu-manu, "the royal guardian," should have the honor of announcing the last commands of Kamehameha to the heir.

It was a dramatic occasion. The tall and handsome Liholiho, flanked by high chiefs, the beautiful Dowager Queen, who spoke as follows, addressing the young King:

"O, heavenly one, I speak to you the commands of your... (father). Here are the chiefs; here are the people of your ancestors; here are your guns; here are your lands. But we two shall share the rule over the land."*

---

* It has been said that Ka-'ahu-manu arrogated this power to herself on the King's death. If so, none at the "wake" dared to challenge her.

After the old king's death, it was Ka-'ahu-manu and Ke-opu-o-lani, with the reluctant consent of the young King, who broke the ancient restrictions of the old religion, and it was Ka-'ahu-manu who decreed the destruction of the images and the heiaus. In the following year, 1820, the *Thaddeus* appeared off Kona with the first company of missionaries from Boston, bringing a new religion to replace the old.

Ka-'ahu-manu did not welcome the missionaries. She had abolished the traditional restrictions and was not about to accept new ones of the New England puritanical type. Her power was growing as the court moved first to Lahaina and then to Honolulu, where one of the triumphant periods of Ka-'ahu-manu's life began.

She fell deeply in love with and married the King of Kaua'i. King Ka-umu-ali'i was a chief of highest rank, the son of Ka-'eo, the grandson of Ke-kau-like, and the still powerful ruler of the Island. This dynastic marriage was also a love match, but it did not prevent Ka-'ahu-manu from also marrying shortly thereafter the King's son and heir, Ke-ali'i-a-ho-nui.

The missionaries were shocked, but the people loved their Queen. For them, she could do no wrong, and by the standards of ali'i of her day and traditionally, plural marriages were neither sinful nor illegal.

The great happiness of their Queen in this period was a joy to the people. They called her "The New Ka-'ahu-manu." She toured every island and was greeted warmly by chiefs and people. They entertained her with affection and deep aloha. She placed her brother on Kaua'i as governor; another brother was already governor of Hawai'i. Her father was succeeded as governor of Maui by Hoapili, her brother-in-law.

Then, a series of tragedies came to darken this time of triumph. Queen Ke-opu-o-lani died at Lahaina in 1823. Early in 1824, her husband Ka-umu-ali-i passed away, and only a month after that her adopted children, Kamehameha II and his young queen, died in London. Christian services were held for all these royal funerals, and it was in this period that Ka-'ahu-manu asked to be instructed in the "Christ life."

Suddenly she was giving public endorsement to the new religion. She went to church. She knelt at the altar. Full aid and cooperation was promised. Ka-'ahu-manu had at last surrendered herself and her people to the Christian faith. Other chiefs on Maui, Kaua'i, and Hawai'i followed her lead as did thousands of her people.

Her power did not end with the death of Kamehameha II. She became the guardian, Regent of the Kingdom, during the minority of the eleven-year-old Kamehameha III. She had declared on the departure of Kamehameha II for England: "The Kingdom is now in my hands and my word is the law of the land. Listen, ye therefore, to my commands. This is the voice of Ka-'ahu-manu!" And so it was.

As Regent, she seemed to recover her old strength. She successfully resisted the impending revolt of Boki, guided the young King, and struggled against the evil forces which were destroying her people. The Reverend Hiram Bingham became her close spiritual guide and advisor.

Queen Ka-'ahu-manu often returned to Maui even after the court had moved to Honolulu, where affairs of state required her residence. The people of Lahaina and of all Maui turned out to honor their Queen with feasts and entertainments. When King Ka-umu-ali'i died in 1824, she arranged for him the Christian burial he desired—not on Kaua'i, the island he loved, but in the cemetery of the Waine'e Church at Lahaina.

Widowed the second time, the Dowager Queen, still Regent for Kamehameha III, during one of her sojourns on Maui, visited Wailuku, where she attended services in a temporary structure serving as a church. She asked that when a new church should be completed, it would be named for her: This is the beautiful old Kaahumanu Church (built 1876) in Wailuku, restored in 1975 to its original beauty.

One of the missionaries described a public meeting in Lahaina in September 1824, just a year after the death of Ke-opu-o-lani, at which Ka-'ahu-manu "called forward three young men belonging to her private school, informed us she had appointed them teachers for her people on the windward side of Maui, and desired that they might be supplied with books sufficient for large schools. She then addressed herself to the headmen of that district who were present, commanding them to have good schoolhouses erected immediately, and to order all the people in her name to attend to the *palapala*, and the *pule*."

At the same time, the Queen pronounced the *Lua-ehu* laws at Lahaina. These were the first written laws under the Hawaiian Kingdom and were proclaimed against murder, theft, boxing, fighting, and desecration of the Sabbath by work or play.

Eight years later, in February 1832, Ka-'ahu-manu sailed for Maui aboard the *Mikapala*. "People from all over Maui had gathered at Lahaina to meet her and construct a fort at this place in order to quell disturbances from the whale ships. In one month it was completed. On this tour, Ka-'ahu-manu met David Malo and said, "I want you to work hard to get an education in order to become an adviser and office holder to administer the affairs of government under my king." After visiting the Big Island, the Queen returned to Lahaina where she and Hoapili, still governor of Maui, set forth additional new laws to protect the government, abolish prostitution, and require legal marriage. Hoapili was then the husband of Ka-'ahu-manu's sister who also was a widowed queen of Kamehameha. Their marriage was the first Christian marriage to be performed among the chiefs.

THE "SACRED" WIFE

Ke-opu-o-lani was the last of the great *niau-pio* chiefs of all Hawai'i. She is called the Sacred Queen in the history books, although the English word "sacred" is not strictly accurate. In the old Hawaiian system she was the highest ranking chief.

She was born at Wailuku on Maui about 1778 of the paramount line of Ke-kau-like, her great-grandfather, and was thus the grand niece of the Maui kings who followed him.

In order to understand the position of a sacred ali'i in the old Hawaiian scheme of things, it is necessary to describe the background in some detail. All the highest ali'i chiefs were considered of divine origin and were literally treated as sacred in their persons.

However, in the Hawaiian way, those chiefs born of brother-sister unions were considered most sacred of all, and these unions were carried out especially to assure the succession to royal power and to obtain the intensified mana important to community and family.

Kamehameha, though related to high chiefs of both the royal lines of Hawai'i and Maui, was not a sacred ali'i. Thus, for dynastic reasons–in other words, to secure the succession of royal power to his children–he took to wife the most sacred princess, Ke-opu-o-lani, who bore him two sons and one daughter. The sons, as is well known, became the heirs to the kingdom established by their father. They were chosen above all other offspring of Kamehameha from the time of their births and were treated as sacred ali'i by the Hawaiian chiefs and people.

Ke-opu-o-lani was the daughter of Kiwala'o and Ke-kui-apo-iwa, son and daughter of Maui's Queen Ka-lola and Hawai'i's King Ka-lani-'opu'u. Kiwala'o was betrothed to his own sister, and Ke-opu-o-lani was born of this union. This type of brother-sister union involved the *Ho ao* ceremony. From birth the couple was carefully guarded; both were virgins; they were taken to the heiau at the chosen time and from evening until dawn remained in a tent-like house fashioned of finest white tapa. All the populace was present, and the chanting of the genealogies (*mo-o-ku-aa-hau*) of the youth and maiden were recounted.

All this was under the direction of the *kahunas* (priests and teachers). At dawn the couple came out of the house erected on the heiau, and the youth was free to go. His sister was carefully guarded until time for birth of the child of this union which was for the purpose of keeping the blood lines sacred. Again, everyone gathered around the heiau, the family and all relatives present as before.

Everyone prayed and chanted while the infant was born. The *kahuna-nui* (chief priest) held the infant for all to see. This was to be the future ruler.

In her younger years, Ke-opu-o-lani was carefully guarded, living under the strictest rules. In her middle years, she suffered poor health for a time, and the King ordered human sacrifices at the heiau to bring about her recovery. On the births of her children they were taken from her to be raised by others, as was customary with the ali'i; all except Nahi-'ena-'ena, the princess whom the Queen Mother insisted on keeping.

Ke-opu-o-lani followed the King on his campaigns and lived with him at his various headquarters and courts. Their unions partook of the "sacred" character inasmuch as the King deferred to this Queen in any matter involving rank, always recognizing her rank as superior to that of his own. For example, Kamehameha was said to approach Ke-opu-o-lani's quarters on his knees, and because of their higher rank, referred to his own children by Ke-opu-o-lani as his grandchildren.

Iolani Liholiho, her oldest son, became Kamehameha II; the younger son, Kau-i-ke-aouli, ruled as Kamehameha III from 1825 to 1854, the longest rule in Hawaiian history. Their sister, Nahi-'ena-'ena, was victim to the confusion of the radical changes in religion and custom brought about by western influences, especially the missionaries. She was pulled in the direction of the old religion by her rank, her upbringing, and the worship of her followers, while being strongly under the influence of the Christian missionaries whom her dying mother had asked to care for her.

FUNERALS AT LAHAINA, 1823-1825

Kamehameha died in 1819 and was the last king to be interred according to the old religion. He was a deeply religious man and faithfully maintained worship of the war god, Ku-'ka'ili-moku, whose care he had inherited from his foster father and uncle, Ka-lani-'opu'u. However, the King forbade, in this case, the human sacrifices normally a part of the ritual of invocation of Ku-'ka'ili-moku, saying, in reference to Liholiho, "The men are sacred to the King."

By 1823, Queen Mother Ke-opu-o-lani was at Lahaina with her second husband, whom Kamehameha had given the name Hoapili ("Bosom Companion"), asking him to act as the guardian of his (Kamehameha's) wives. The adoption of Christianity by High Chief Hoapili and the sacred Dowager Queen was the first big step forward for the young New England missionaries.

THE DEATH OF KE-OPU-O-LANI

Queen Ke-opu-o-lani died in 1823, not long after the establishment of the mission at Lahaina. There is a woodcut which shows the funeral procession in silhouette, the coffin borne on the shoulders of the chiefs, the King Liholiho following, and her two younger children carried on the shoulders of their *kahus*. It was a sad loss for the missionaries, as it was for the Hawaiians and their royal family; saddest of all for the children.

As with the death of Kamehameha, which marked the end of the old era, the death of his "sacred wife," literally in the arms of the new religion, marked the beginning of a new era in Hawai'i.

It was to be an era of rapid and drastic change. When the wailing for the departed Queen Ke-opu-o-lani, his sacred mother, had died away, Liholiho, King Kamehameha II, decided to visit the King of England. He took with him his half-sister and favorite wife and a small retinue of chiefs and retainers. The King designated his young brother, Kau-i-ke-aouli, as his successor and Ka-'ahu-manu as regent. Kau-i-ke-aouli and his sister, the Princess Nahi-'ena-'ena, continued to live in Lahaina, there to receive the homage of chiefs and people while studying their letters and religion.

In 1824, the chiefs decided to share the *palapala* with the people, especially those who attended them. In 1824, the Princess, a beautiful child of nine, together with her stepfather Hoapili, presided over her own school which had that year an enrollment of two hundred and seventy children.

That same year brought still another royal funeral to "Lahaina of the breadfruit leaves," "the land of the chiefs." This was the royal funeral of the gentle Ka-umu-ali'i, son of the great Maui and Kaua'i chiefs.

The two royal children seemed happy there for a time; then suffered another blow. Their brother and half sister, the King and Kamamalu, died of the measles in London in 1824. Their bodies were returned to Hawai'i by the British Government in H.M.S. *Blonde*, under command of Lord Byron, cousin of the poet.

"When the ship reached Lahaina on May 4, 1825, the little Princess, Rev. Richards, and Hoapili paced up and down the beach waiting for the landing party. As it approached, Hoapili seated himself on a chair in the sand, while Richards with the Princess leaning at his side, stood at the Chief's left. The people gathered in large numbers, thronged across the entire beach and began to wail.

"When the landing party touched the shore and started to walk up the sand, a passage was opened through the people for them to approach the chiefs. Hoapili rose from his chair, and with a great roar of wailing, held out his arms to Liliha, his daughter, who was the first ranking chief to step out of the ship's boat. The Princess in her turn, sprang from Richards' side and ran to Liliha's arms; meanwhile the chiefs, led by Hoapili in an ancient custom, knelt down and rubbed their faces in the sand.

"The wailing mounted, drowning out the noise of the sea until Richards became concerned over the possibility of violence in the midst of this display of grief for the dead monarchs. He suggested to Nahi-'ena-'ena that they pray to Jehovah in the hope that a religious ceremony would diminish the surge of feeling and curb the rising confusion. She passed the suggestion to Boki, and mats were spread for prayer. This simple action brought quiet to the crowd."

The bodies of the King and Queen were brought ashore and carried to the small island of Moku'ula, a tabu spot sacred to the chiefs, where they remained lying in state until the *Blonde* was made ready for the trip to Honolulu. The chiefs went aboard for the sad journey to Honolulu, accompanied by Hoapili, Nahi-'ena-'ena, and Kau-i-ke-aouli, the Prince, now to become King Kamehameha the Third.

THE SISTER OF THE KING

Since the time of her birth, the subject of Nahi-'ena-'ena's marriage to her brother had been discussed by the chiefs. It was to be expected that the missionaries would disapprove of such a marriage for their little Princess on both religious and biological grounds. The problem, however, was not only an ethical or biological one or even one caused by the necessity of breeding future royalty. The two children had been brought up together; they had been paired from the time of the Princess' birth, and a great devotion existed between them. It was a cultural and psychological reality that in Hawai'i royal brothers and sisters were often very close to each other. Such attachments appear in many of the old legends and chants.

The chiefs consulted the missionaries in 1824 about the propriety of a union between Nahi-'ena-'ena and Kau-i-ke-aouli. One of the missionaries consulted, Elisha Loomis, wrote: "It is well known here that the Prince and Princess for a considerable time past have lived in a state of incest. This would appear extraordinary in America as the Prince is but ten years of age and the Princess less than seven or eight. It should be remembered, however, that persons arrive at the age of puberty here much sooner than in a colder climate. Chastity is not a recommendation; the sexes associating without restraint almost from infancy."

The devotion between the young King and his sister, deepened by their isolation as sacred ali'i and as children early bereaved of their parents and brother and sister, deepened further and intensified as they grew into maturity. At the same time, Nahi-'ena-'ena's devotion to the new religion, as taught her by the Reverends Stewart and Richards, increased. She was ever reminded of her mother's dying wish that she live the life of a Christian. She was admitted to the church at Lahaina in January 1827. She was baptized in company of some of her attendants and received the Lord's Supper.

"She took the name, Harriet, or Harieta, which her mother had chosen in tribute to the friendship of Mrs. Stewart, the missionary's wife...Charles Stewart, her devoted teacher and his wife were not present on this occasion; because of the illness of his wife they had left Hawai'i in 1825. William Richards was now the Princess' mentor at the mission."

The Reverend Richards and the Princess made two memorable tours of Maui. These were for the purpose of visiting the schools and churches and encouraging the *palapala* and the *pule*. These tours were greatly enhanced by the presence of Nahi-'ena-'ena, who was received everywhere in the Island with reverence and joy.

Richards climbed to the crater, rejoining the Princess at Kahului for the canoe trip along the north shore. Everywhere the Princess spoke to the people, and Richards was most impressed with her address at Kaupo, where she said: "Formerly we [the chiefs] were the terror of the country–when visiting your district–we should have perhaps bidden you erect an heiau and after being worn out with this labor, we should have sacrificed you in it. Now we bring you the *palapala*–the word of God–why should you fear it?"

"But Nahi-'ena-'ena was by now growing weary with the necessity of examining the state of her soul," she was physically mature and longed for the adulation which was hers as a highborn ali'i. Furthermore, many of the chiefs were her companions and instructors in dancing, singing, drinking, and card playing. She was more often in Honolulu, taking part in all important occasions as the partner of her brother, who in this period was himself prone to drown his sorrows in strong drink.

His sister was often swept up in the activities of Kau-i-ke-aouli's increasingly dissolute court, returning to Lahaina off and on to seek repentance and attend to her school and her religious duties. In October 1830, she took up residence in the Richards' home and made valiant efforts to resist the pull of Honolulu and her desire for her beloved brother, the King.

In the end, she returned to the ways of the dissolute court, and not even the Richards could get her to return. In 1834, the union of Nahi-'ena-'ena and the King was announced formally in Honolulu by a crier sent throughout the city.

She returned to Lahaina in 1835, alternately attending religious services and seeking the help of the Reverend Andrews and her old teacher, Richards, and failing back into her old ways and into spells of depression. In 1835, she was married at the Waine'e church to a young chief, Lele-io-hoku. The Reverend Richards performed the ceremony.

"The last year of her life [1836] was one of illness, confusion and dejection. The King came to Lahaina and the brother and sister again took up a life of revelry and there were brief times when she escaped from the darkness and madness in her heart. She gave birth to a child; the infant, a son, lived only a few hours. After the birth she remained gravely ill and died at the end of December 1836."

Nahi-'ena-'ena's funeral was the last of the burials of Hawaiian royalty at Lahaina. "Chiefs and commoners lamented for the Chiefess whose children they had hoped to see carry on the line of ruling chiefs." Her brother was grief stricken. "He escorted his sister's remains on board a warship fitted out to carry her in state to the tomb of their mother. In Lahaina a royal roadway was constructed from the shore to the place of burial, and the funeral was celebrated in pomp with a fine procession. 'This last funeral and service of prayer concluded the weeping and lamentation of the chiefs and people of Maui for their beloved Princess.' As for Kau-i-ke-aouli, such was his love and regret for his sister that he continued to live on Maui for eight years…He made the day of his sister's death a public holiday, ordered guns to be fired from the government forts from Hawai'i to Kaua'i, and gave big feasts every year in its celebration."

The King was shocked and sobered into taking stock in the state of his Kingdom. He went on to become one of Hawai'i's most distinguished monarchs.

DEATH OF KA-'AHU-MANU

The "Favorite Wife," Ka-'ahu-manu–the extraordinary woman born in a cave at Hana who rose to be, after her husband the Conqueror, Hawai'i's greatest leader died in 1832. She was sixty-four.

Her death was more a triumph than a tragedy. Chiefs and commoners from all the islands gathered to sing their Queen to sleep. She was borne by retainers and chiefs to her home in the Manoa Valley beyond Honolulu.

At the end, she died secure in her love of the Christian God. She was buried in the Royal Tomb at Nu'uanu with the rituals of the new religion so different from the funeral ceremonies of Kamehameha only thirteen years earlier.

In so many ways during those few years the old order of Hawaiian life itself had changed.

CHAPTER 7

CHIEFS, WHALERS, AND MISSIONARIES: 1820-1860

Once more we sail with a northerly gale
Towards our island home.
Our main mast sprung and our whaling done,
And we ain't got far to roam.
We're homeward bound from the Arctic ground,
Rolling down to old Maui.

> —Sung by American whaling men in the nineteenth
> century, this chantey anticipated the sailor's
> long-awaited return to Maui's Lahaina Roads.

You are to aim at covering these islands with
ruitful fields and pleasant dwellings, and schools
and churches, and raising up the whole people to
an elevated state of Christian civilization.

> – From the instructions to the American missionaries
> from the American Board of Commissioners for Foreign Missions.

The developments at Lahaina in the first half of the nineteenth century were so dramatic and bizarre as to stir the imagination. From a sleepy Hawaiian village, long the favorite watering place of the ali'i and many times the battleground of the chiefly wars, Lahaina became for a short time the political and cultural center of the newly-developing kingdom of Hawai'i. At the same time, this village of grass houses with its fine protected roadstead, together with Honolulu, became the very center of the whaling industry of the Pacific, a port famed among seamen for its grog shops and its lusty women, and by the sea captains as a winter haven to prepare for the long, arduous voyages to the very edges of the lonely Pacific Ocean in search of whales.

It is a strange coincidence that the whalers and the missionaries, both of them coming as they did mainly from the New England coast of the United States, should have met head on in this remote Pacific town beyond the Horn* on the western shore of the Island of Maui.

Long before these Yankees found themselves working at cross purposes in Lahaina, perhaps five hundred years before, the Polynesian ali'i selected Lahaina as a place for good living and relaxation. The long beach was warm, and the gentle waves off the reef were perfectly formed for the surfing which the chiefs so much enjoyed.

The whole area around Lahaina was well-watered by streams of fresh water flowing profusely out of the West Maui Mountains. These fresh, cool waters caused the plain of Lahaina to flourish in the hot sun with all kinds of tropical growth, with sugar cane, breadfruit, coconut, and banana. This same water filled the walled taro patches from streams and canals to produce the excellent taro of Maui.

William Ellis wrote in his journal in 1823: "The appearance of Lahaina from the anchorage is singularly romantic and beautiful. A fine sandy beach stretches along the margin of the sea, lined for a considerable distance with houses, and adorned with shady clumps of Kou trees, or waving groves of cocoanuts…"

Those same streams provided the fresh water so essential to the merchantmen and whalers who found refreshment there in increasing numbers after 1820.

THE PELELEU FLEET

At the turn of the century, Kamehameha had decided to build an immense fleet primarily for the invasion of Kaua'i, but also as a means of keeping his warriors busy with the promise of conquering more lands. A young supercargo on board the *Neptune*, an American sealing ship anchored off Kawaiahae in August 1798, was befriended by the King. His name was Ebenezer Townsend, Jr. He wrote in his diary, "…while we lay there, I proposed learning him (he spelled the King's name Amaiamai-ah) the compass, which I had some reason

---

*The saying among the whalers was, "There is no God beyond the Horn."

to regret, for he kept me at it continually until he learned it." He watched Kamehameha's skilled canoe makers finishing the seventy-foot long war canoes that were called *wa'a peleleu*.

He was told that the Hawaiians could paddle these canoes at nine knots, and he was impressed by their fine workmanship. At the same time two white men were building a brick house at Lahaina for the King, who told young Townsend that he intended to reside there part of the time.

In 1802, Kamehameha moved his *peleleu* fleet (said by Kamakau to have had 800 canoes) first to Kipahulu and Kaupo, where heiaus were erected and their tabu declared by the young prince, Liholiho—then only five years old but already proclaimed as heir to the kingdom. They then went on to Lahaina from Kaupo where they remained about a year, "feed-hag and clothing themselves with the wealth of Maui, Moloka'i, Lana'i, Kaho'olawe, and worshiping the gods." It was while the expedition was encamped at Lahaina that Ka-me'e-ia-moku, one of the four chief counselers of the kingdom and the father of Hoapili, died at Pu'uki, Lahaina.

It is said that before he became too weak Kamehameha went to see him. He turned and kissed the cheek and said, "I have something to tell you. Ka-hekili was your father; you were not Keoua's son; here are the tokens that you are the son of Ka-hekili." The chief said, "Strange, that you should live all this time and only when dying tell me that I am Ka-hekili's son. Had you told me this before my brothers need not have died. They could have ruled Maui while I ruled Hawai'i." Ka-me'e-ia-moku answered, "That is not a good thought. If they lived, there would have been constant warfare between you. With you alone as ruler the country is at peace."

Kamehameha's brick palace was on the point at Lahaina just in front of where the present library is located. It was the very center of the long encampment which lasted during the year 1802. There were so many chiefs and retainers that the thatched dwellings and taro patches stretched as far as the war canoes. The retinue including the households of the King's children was estimated at a thousand persons.

The year in Lahaina was a year of peace and relaxation. Walls of taro fields which had been destroyed in earlier wars were repaired, and the rich land was generally made productive again. House lots and taro fields in Lahaina were given by Kamehameha to some of his favorites. Instead of roads they used the little pathways that were formed by the tops of the stone walls around the taro fields, slightly raised and kept in excellent condition. In 1803 Kamehameha moved his fleet to O'ahu. Before his departure the King received from Captain Cleveland of the *Lelia Byrd* a horse and mare. He learned to ride and became an excellent horseman. The horse created a sensation in Hawai'i. Soon all the chiefs followed the King's lead in acquiring horses. Horseback riding became the most popular sport in Hawai'i, and roads were built to accommodate horse-drawn vehicles.

The *peleleu* fleet never reached Kaua'i. In 1803, a plague struck O'ahu. The King survived but many died. Another attempt was defeated by a storm which turned back the fleet. In 1810, Ka-umu-ali'i agreed to making the Kaua'i kingdom tributary to the Kamehameha dynasty, and the beautiful canoes were left to rot on the beaches at Waikiki. They had served their purpose and had, besides, become obsolete as the King had acquired modern sailing vessels armed with modern artillery.

WHALING: LAHAINA 1820-1860

Even before Kamehameha's death, Lahaina began to develop as an economic center, first as a point of supply for visiting ships and then as a port for the loading of sandalwood. Lahaina also offered a desirable port of call for the trans-Pacific traffic in furs. The business of provisioning the whaling fleet began in 1819 when the first whale ships visited Hawai'i. When, for political reasons, the capital was moved to Honolulu and the whaling industry declined, Lahaina became once again a drowsy village on a sun-drenched beach, and progress passed it by.

However, during the middle part of the nineteenth century, Lahaina became for a time the whaling capital of the world. The first two whale ships which arrived in 1819 had increased to a hundred by 1824, and by 1829 one hundred and seventy whale ships had visited Hawai'i. In the period 1829-1849, twenty years, the number doubled, and then almost doubled again, and the whole industry moved northward from equatorial seas to the Sea of Japan, the Arctic, and Hawai'i.

The impact on Lahaina of the whaling business at its height was intense. The Reverend Dwight Baldwin, medical missionary at Lahaina, wrote: "Ten days since we had two whale ships, next day ten came in, and the next day six. From that time to this, scarce an hour but we have seen from one to half a dozen coming down the channel—fifty ships now here."

During the early spring and fall from the early 1820s through the 1860s this pattern was repeated and Lahaina Roads became the principal anchorage of America's whaling fleet. The town became the recruiting grounds for supplies and Hawaiian seamen, a great many of whom, in those days, began signing up as whalers or able seamen on the many ships coming in. In 1846, Lahaina's peak year, 429 whale ships arrived there compared to 167 which anchored at Honolulu.

At that time, Lahaina was a town of 3,000 people, 59 stone or wooden houses, and 882 grass houses. Lahaina Roads offered ships the following advantages enumerated by a contemporary observer: "The anchorage being an open roadstead, vessels can always approach or leave it with any wind that blows. No pilot is needed here. Vessels generally approach through the channel between Maui and Moloka'i, standing well over to Lana'i, as far as the trade will carry them, then take the sea breeze which sets in during the forenoon, and head for town. The anchorage is about ten miles in extent along the shore and from within a cable's length of the reef in seven fathoms of water, to a distance of three miles out with some twenty-five fathoms, affording abundant room for as large a fleet as can ever be collected here."

Each ship was boarded by the harbor master, who presented the captain with a copy of the regulations. It said in part: "Every master of a foreign vessel who desires the privilege of purchasing refreshments for his vessel at Lahaina, shall pay to the harbor master, ten dollars, in return for which said master shall be entitled to receive five barrels of potatoes, with the privilege of purchasing at pleasure in the market supplies for his ship, according to the rules of the place."

The Reverend Dr. Baldwin wrote that the chief food items supplied to the ships were "water, hogs, goats, bananas, mellons, pumpkins, onions, squashes, sweet potatoes, young turkeys, ducks, fowls, and beef, all of which can be had in abundance; but the greatest article for which they come is Irish potatoes which grow plentifully in the interior of this island." Irish potatoes, grown mostly at Kula, were a drawing card for Lahaina as a whaling station. The American sailors much preferred them to the yams of Oʻahu.

Fresh water was one of the most important commodities supplied to the whalers at Lahaina. The process of procuring water was described by one of the whaling captains as follows: "It was the custom for the whale ships to land the casks to be filled with water upon the beach, then the kanakas [native men]... would roll them to the watering place and, after filling, roll them back to the beach and raft them off to the boats."

Lahaina also offered the whalers recreation. As several whaling captains pointed out in a letter to the government, "The life of a whaler is one of hardship and toil, and upon his arrival at your port, he needs rest and relaxation...'tis absolutely necessary to the lives of the sailors that they should have liberty days..." It was over what were considered the necessary ingredients of a sailor's "rest and relaxation" that the missionaries and government officials disagreed with the whalers and the owners of the brothels and grog shops which catered to them.

They carried on a continuing feud which burst into violence from time to time. The first serious Lahaina riot broke out in October 1825, when the crew of the English whaler *Daniel*, angered by a new law passed by the chiefs prohibiting women from visiting the ships, roamed the streets menacingly for three days. They twice threatened the home and lives of the Reverend William Richards and his wife, believing them to be the instigators of the law.

The riot of 1827 was also started by an English whaler, this time under command of an American, Captain Clark. Governor

Hoapili, finding that some women had broken the tabu and gone aboard the whaler *John Palmer*, seized Captain Clark's boat and would not let him go back to his ship until the women had been returned. Captain Clark told his mate that if he had not been released within an hour, the ship should fire upon the town. Clark promised to return the women and was released, but before he could reach his ship, the *John Palmer* began firing. Apparently the cannon were aimed directly at the mission house for the cannon balls landed in the yard. When Clark boarded his ship the firing ceased; but he sailed away to Honolulu without returning the women.

Much of the problem of maintaining law and order in the town of Lahaina centered around the control of liquor, a problem in which the whaling captains shared, as a letter from several of the captains to Governor Hoapili of Maui shows: "We do not any of us like to go to Oʻahu, because bad men sell rum to our seamen. We like your island, because you have a good law preventing the sale of this poison. But now, after lying here in peace for some weeks, a vessel has come among us from Oʻahu with rum for sale. Our seamen are drinking it, and trouble is commencing. We now look to you for protection."

In 1843, while the islands were temporarily ceded under duress to Great Britain, grog shops were licensed and rioting flared up again. "A party of half-drunken sailors went to the King to take him. The King's people returned the sailors" stones with great fury and one of his attendants knocked the leader senseless to the ground. After the riot was dispersed, he was taken to the fort–but the war went on. A chief on horseback was assailed by the sailors with stones–the natives flew to his aid, and stones flew on both sides–some skulls supposed to be broken but none have yet proved fatal. Toward evening as the seamen gathered toward the landing, war, noise, oaths, obscenity, and hurled stones filled the air–but a party armed with swords by the authority, somewhat moderated the rage of the sailors."

In 1845, the constable of Lahaina complained, "There are so many Beer shops here, and they have so many chances of selling spirits in their Beer without detection that, do all I can, and use all the means in my power, I cannot get a fair chance to fine them…"

One of the most famous sailors to arrive at Lahaina was Herman Melville, who arrived on April 26, 1843, aboard the *Charles and Henry*, a whaling ship owned by the Coffins of Nantucket. Melville took his discharge at Lahaina, then sailed on the *Star* for Honolulu. His departure was well-timed, for the week after his departure, the *Acushnet*, which he had deserted in the Marquesas, dropped anchor at Lahaina. One of the first things that Captain Pease did was to go to the United States Commercial Agent to report, "Richard T. Green and Herman Melville deserted at Nukuhiva, July 9, 1842."

HOAPILI, GOVERNOR OF MAUI: 1823-1840

Among those who stood fast against the outrages of the whalermen was High Chief Hoapili. Intimate of Kamehameha I, he had been an early convert to Christianity. After the King's death he had married Ke-opu-o-lani and, after her death, he had married another high-ranking widow of the King, a sister of Ka-'ahu-manu. She took the name of her husband in the Christian manner and was always afterward referred to as Hoapili-wahine (Mrs. Hoapili). Governor of Maui from 1823 until his death, he had, despite frequent and difficult opposition, maintained a reasonably stable and peaceable authority. He also had a powerful influence on the development of the new religion, education, the laws of the new kingdom, as well as its political, social and cultural development.

A confidant of both Kamehameha II and especially of Kamehameha III, the latter was with him at the time of his death on January 2, 1840.

The missionary report for the Lahaina station spoke of the good faith of Hoapili and his good works "…his sense of obligation to Christ for renewal and pardon of sin, his longing to be gone, that none of us could mistake the meaning. Though in his last extremity, Hoapili rose upon his knees, which to us seemed impossible, and then poured out his soul to God. When through he said, 'napau' ["It is done"]. His anxiety for the future welfare of this nation, his warn-

ings and entreaties to the King [Kamehameha III, then aged 29 and
at the height of his dissolute period], and the tears he poured out
over him were almost as much as his majesty could endure…We
need not add, that we remember him with affection and interest and
that we greatly deplore his loss as a civil ruler. The Lord raise up
many such to preside over this perishing people. There was no wailing at the funeral as Hoapili had forbidden it." The report is not
signed but was obviously written by Baldwin.

Hoapili's good works included the building of the Waine'e Church
where, at his request, he was buried next to the grave of the Reverend
Charles McDonald, a young teacher who had died the year before.

For a time after the death of Hoapili, grog shops and brothels
openly plied their trade, and the chiefs who replaced him, as well as
the haole commissioners, were more interested in making money
than saving souls or maintaining strict adherence to the regulations.

However, the temperance movement was gaining ground,
and in September 1846 forty people had signed the temperance
pledge, including captains and seamen. Apparently there were some
setbacks as indicated in a letter to Boston in December written by
Dr. Baldwin: "A few nights since after midnight our police hauled
out at the windows at the lodging place of one firm of our merchants eleven young Hawaiian girls who had sold themselves to
pollution, slaves to the Devil and their own lusts. One of this firm
was our late deputy consul who came out with Mr. Abel. Another
proprietor was our present deputy consul who came out with Judge
Terrill, his in-law; a third was a professor of religion with respect-
able connections from New York. Oh tempera!!"

The New Learning

Despite the turmoil often resulting from the whaling trade at
Lahaina, it simultaneously became the center of education for the
Hawaiian Kingdom.

It was also here that the planning took place which led to the
enactment of many of the kingdom's first laws. One of these

required that all persons under twenty-six who wished to marry must prove their ability to read and write. This, coupled with strict laws prohibiting sex outside of marriage, led to a remarkable level of literacy!

The *palapala* (writing) and the *pule* (prayer) went hand in hand with the new religious instruction. The first school in Lahaina began in the year 1823. The Reverend Stewart wrote, "Monday, June 2nd, our school has been commenced." This was the school of Queen Ke-opu-o-lani, so that she could learn the *palapala*. At the age of fifty-five, according to the Reverend Richards, one of her teachers, she was "indeed a diligent pupil seldom weary with studies, and often spent hours over her little spelling book."

Then, Ka-'ahu-manu, a year later at Lahaina, proclaimed that, "When schools are established, all the people shall learn the *palapala*." During Ka-'ahu-manu's reign as premier, schools sprang up everywhere. These were native grass houses without benches or shelves. All of the pupils sat upon mats. "The *ali'i* scholars were of both sexes and all ages. The teacher blew a shell when it was time for school to assemble, which was about three in the afternoon." By 1832 schools for native children began. By 1835 the mission press in Honolulu had printed 16,000 primers. Five years later, twenty-two textbooks had been printed in the Hawaiian language.

LAHAINALUNA SCHOOL

According to Kuykendall, Lahainaluna high school "was, without a doubt, the most important school in the Hawaiian Islands during the reign of Kamehameha III." It was opened in September 1831 and was the first high school west of the Rocky Mountains. One of the dormitories was named for Hoapili, who, with his wife, had given 1,000 acres of land for its establishment.

The Reverend Andrews and his sixty adult students built the first house of stones, but it fell during a heavy storm. They built a second house of stones and timber. The logs were dragged from the forests of East Maui over a distance of thirty-five miles to Ma'alaea

Bay, where they were placed in canoes and brought to Lahaina. The haole missionaries marveled at the industriousness and capacity for hard work exhibited by the Hawaiians. Even the chiefs took part, as they had done in the past when building a heiau or preparing the taro fields. King and court were once observed by the missionaries singing as they walked into the town covered with mud from their labors in the royal taro patch near Lahaina.

The report of the Minister of Public Instruction for 1850 stated that Lahainaluna "has sent out over 400 educated Hawaiians...they are now the leading men of the native population all over the islands."

At this time, the United States consisted of twenty-three states, there were only nine high schools, and book learning for all the people was frowned upon in America and Europe. Several years later, the printing house, Hale Pa'i, an old coralstone building still in existence, was built by the missionaries who founded Lahainaluna. It was in this building on February 14, 1834, that the first newspaper west of the Rockies was printed. It was called *Kalama Hawaii*, or "Torch of Hawai'i."

When, by 1841, public education had progressed to the point where a school inspector was needed, David Malo, a graduate of Lahainaluna School, was named Superintendent of Education for Maui, Lana'i, and Moloka'i. His first report, dated April 1841, stated that there were ten schools with ten teachers and five hundred and thirty-seven scholars at Lahaina.

An important part of the development of education as well as religion, and the political development of the kingdom, is attributed to King Kamehameha III. On October 10, 1840, he signed the final draft of the first written Hawaiian Constitution. This act was performed by the King at Lahaina.

RIKEKE

Kamakau, in his *Ruling Chiefs,* wrote that, "The Hawaiian people believed in William Richards (Rikeke), the foreigner who taught the King to change the government of the Hawaiian people to a constitutional monarchy and end that of a supreme ruler, and his views were adopted."

One cannot read the diaries of these Lahaina missionaries without recognizing the qualities which they brought to their religious and educational mission to Maui. Richards was one of the best. When he and his wife had to go to the States because of the health of Mrs. Richards and the children, David Malo wrote a long letter to their church in Northampton, Massachusetts, fearing the church might persuade them not to return. Malo wrote: "…he has ever dwelt in the midst of us laboring constantly day and night, taking no rest from his toils during the whole period of his dwelling with us, forever seeking the good of these Sandwich Islands.

William Richards' career was most closely connected with Maui. The teacher of the Queen Ke-opu-o-lani, a founder of the school system and of the Lahainaluna School, the staunch friend of the Hawaiian people, his unusual qualities were recognized by the youthful Kamehameha III as he sought to establish a stable kingdom in the Islands.

Richards was a brave man. He defied the drunken whale-men who several times threatened his life and that of his wife, who once stood courageously forth to challenge a riotous crowd and to protect her husband.

He was also a scholar and a man of great spiritual strength. Richards translated, with David Malo's help, several books of the Bible into Hawaiian. He preached and taught and fully practiced the Christian way. He ministered to the poor and the downtrodden as well as to the ali'i.

Kamehameha III appointed William Richards to two very important positions. He was translator and special advisor to the King, and he became Hawai'i's first Minister of Education. He is also known in Hawaiian history for the Richards-Ha'alilio Mission. Accompanied by the brilliant young secretary of the King, Timothy Ha'alilio, Richards was sent to Washington, London, and Paris, there to secure guarantees of the independence of the Hawaiian Kingdom which was being bullied by high-handed, self-appointed representatives of the British government in Honolulu.

Richards and Ha'alilio were successful in their diplomatic mission and thereby performed a service of the greatest significance for Hawai'i since it helped in preserving the independence of the kingdom.

Unfortunately, the fine chief, Ha'alilio, died on the long voyage home. Richards returned to continue his service as Minister of Education until his death in 1847. He was buried at Lahaina near the tomb of his first royal pupil, Queen Ke-opu-o-lani, in the cemetery by the church whose name was changed from Waine'e to Waiola ("The Waters of Life").

THE MEDICAL MISSIONARY

No less remarkable in his way was the young Dr. Dwight Baldwin who replaced Richards as the preeminent religious leader at Lahaina. He came there in 1835 from Waimea, where the cold air was felt to be bad for his health. He and his good missionary wife found their life work at Lahaina, Maui. Eight children were born to them there, of whom six lived to people the island with sugar planters, business men, ranchers, farmers, and even a few "Chicken Baldwins," so called because they raised chickens at Kihei.

Dwight Baldwin both preached and treated the sick, often traveling in bad weather for several days to points as far away as Hana or crossing choppy seas to treat a patient on Lana'i or Moloka'i. He was instrumental, with other medical men, in saving Maui from the smallpox which swept O'ahu. He promoted and visited schools. He treated the many who suffered from the measles epidemic and, when rejoicing that none had died from it, was appalled to find many dying in the month after the measles epidemic from a severe diarrhea brought on by eating the foods which had been avoided during the measles period.

Baldwin spoke most highly of David Malo, the Hawaiian missionary and historian. "David Malo has, perhaps, the strongest mind of any man in the nation..."

David Malo is buried in a lonely grave on the summit of Mt. Ball above the Lahainaluna School. It was his request to be buried there away from the white men whom he felt would supersede his race. The missionaries he always upheld, but he had seen too many foreigners of a different type.

THE CATHOLICS

It is said that the first Mass was held on Maui in January 1841 at the home of one Joaquin Armas, a cowboy who worked for King Kamehameha III.

Though strongly opposed by the Protestant missionaries and by the chiefs, especially Queen Regent Ka-'ahu-manu, the Catholics gradually became established on Maui. One local legend has it that the faith was propagated by sailors from a shipwrecked Spanish galleon in the sixteenth century. However, the first known Catholic priest at Lahaina arrived in 1846 and quickly found a large following on the island.

Early converts were Helio and Petero, brothers from Wailua and Wailuku. Helio was baptized in Honolulu and returned to Maui to travel about preaching the Roman Catholic faith. He became known as "The Apostle of Maui" and died at Wailua between Hana and Kaupo where his grave below a peak in the center of Wailua gulch is marked by a twenty-foot cross of concrete. The Maria Lanikula Church was built in 1858 at Lahaina.

One of the most interesting stories of the Catholics on Maui is that of the march from the Kaupo-Kipahulu districts all the way to Wailuku when the judge at Wailuku ordered the Catholics to be arrested. The men who were deputised to arrest and bring them to trial in Wailuku tied them together with ropes and marched them along the Pi'ilani Highway through all the districts of Hana and Nahiku, Kaenae, Kailua, Haiku, and Paia.

They were led by Helio and his brother, and as they went along they were joined by others on the long march to Wailuku. By the time they reached Wailuku there were several hundred–too many, indeed, to be tried, and the judge at Wailuku dismissed the case. Petero and Helio and the others made their way back along the highway, preaching as they went.

The journey of the captive Catholics from Kahiki-nui, Kaupo and Hana, which took more than a month, was called the paakaula ("the tying with ropes"). The result was the tripling of the number of catechumens on Maui, then over a thousand. The Edict of Toleration by Kamehameha III at Lahaina on June 17, 1839, gave religious freedom to his people, and the first Catholic catechism, the Vahi Katekimo, was published in Honolulu in 1847.

St. Anthony's Church, a stone edifice, replaced an earlier frame structure at Wailuku. It was blessed by Bishop Maigret on May 3, 1873. After Mass, the Bishop expressed the hope that one of the priests would volunteer to help the lepers on Moloka'i. Father Damien answered the call and, in time, became the "fellow leper of my little flock." St. Anthony's Church was destroyed by fire on November 1, 1977, and a new structure was built in its place.

THE DECLINE OF WHALING

The peak for the whaling industry in Hawai'i was reached in 1846 when the total number of whale ships reaching Hawaiian ports was almost six hundred. The years 1845 to 1855 were the best, and eight times before 1860 the annual total ship arrivals was more than five hundred. During that period, Hawai'i's total economic dependence on whaling became obvious.

The long decline began in the late fifties. In 1859, oil was discovered in Pennsylvania, and the consequent production of cheap kerosene spelled the doom of whaling. The Civil War just about ruined the whaling fleet. Forty whale ships were taken to the harbor entrances at two of the southern port cities where they were sunk by the Union in an attempt to block off the harbors. The Confederate raider, *Shenandoah*, burned the Hawaiian ship *Harvest* in the Marianas in 1865.

But the final disaster came in 1871 when thirty-three ships, nearly half of them Hawaiian, were trapped in an early freeze in the ice floes north of Bering Strait. The crews escaped, but the ships and cargoes were lost. Five hundred Hawaiian sailors reached home penniless. The cost to Hawaiian whaling interests was at least $200,000, and, to the industry, ten times that much.

With the decline of whaling and the growth of Honolulu as the political capital, the heyday of Lahaina passed. For a time the growth and development of the sugar industry revived the commercial life of Lahaina, but the historic town drowsed in the sun for many decades until the middle of the twentieth century, when Lahaina became a destination, not for thousands, but literally for millions of people.

CHAPTER 8

SUGAR AND WATER

It requires 500,000 gallons of water to produce a ton of sugar.

–Plantation official as quoted in Maui Sun,
December 26-January 1, 1978.

Sugar cane grows wild in Hawai'i. It was introduced by the Polynesians who brought cuttings with them from the South Pacific. When off Maui in 1778, Captain Cook purchased a large quantity of cane from the canoes which surrounded his ships. The brew that he made from the Maui cane and insisted the men drink for its nutritional value very nearly touched off a mutiny on board the *Resolution*. He had substituted "cane beer" for grog, but when the men protested, he reluctantly restored their daily ration of rum and water.

Many of the earliest Chinese residents in Hawai'i were knowledgeable in sugar production, the *tong see* (sugar masters), establishing successful plantations on Maui and Hawai'i. In 1828, two Chinese merchants established the Hungtai sugar works at Wailuku.

During the early part of the nineteenth century many attempts were made to turn Hawai'i's wild cane into a cash crop. A passenger on the *Blonde* in 1825 was a Mr. Dickinson who settled in Manoa Valley on O'ahu, where he established, in cooperation with the O'ahu governor, the High Chief Boki, a sugar cane field and small mill. The mill was moved closer to Honolulu, and the sugar cane was turned into rum, much to the displeasure of the missionaries, the Regent Ka-'ahu-manu, and the Christian chiefs. The latter placed what was, in effect, a kapu on the operation, and the missionaries, by refusing use of their bullock carts (the only means of transporting the cane) effectively put an end to the venture. Ka-'ahu-manu then caused the cane fields to be destroyed.

As whaling declined, efforts were made at the islands to find some industry to replace its prime position in the Hawaiian economy. The missionaries and the traders, as well as the Hawaiians themselves, looked increasingly to the land instead of the sea for answers to this problem. If they were able to develop agricultural products it might overcome the instability of the whaling industry. As Daws put it in his history of Hawai'i, "people would not have to go on thinking of themselves as whoremasters or whalermen."

The idea of agriculture became most attractive when the gold rush in California suddenly brought into being a new market for Hawaiian produce. The timing was excellent. The whaling season of 1847-48 had been very poor, and businessmen in Honolulu and Lahaina were overstocked. Nevertheless, by the end of 1848 the stores had been stripped of everything that might be of use in the gold fields–from pickaxes to playing cards and even Bibles. Many of the white men and hundreds of natives joined the rush to California.

In 1850, the Hawaiian government passed laws permitting aliens to buy land in fee simple. Investors went heavily into debt to buy property and planted crops in anticipation of selling to the West Coast market. "Speculation in sugar was rife as long as the gold rush lasted but when the market failed, disaster followed immediately. The procession of bankruptcies was mournful in the extreme and many planters were shaken out of the business altogether."

Nevertheless, some survived, and by 1860, despite general depressed conditions, the number of plantations had risen to twelve, and all were busy and sugar prices were rising.

Then came the Civil War which, while crippling the whaling industry in the Pacific, proved the making of the Hawaiian sugar industry.

Southern sugar disappeared from the market, and in the northern states of the Union sugar prices climbed high. The planters could sell with profit even after paying the heavy U.S. tariff.

By 1866 there were thirty-two plantations and mills in the Islands, compared with twelve in 1860; one and a half million pounds were exported in 1860, and in 1866 the figure was almost eighteen million pounds.

Planters began to form companies to share the risks. Hackfeld took over Ladd & Company's now bankrupt Koloa Plantation on Kaua'i. Others were formed by Castle & Cooke and C. Brewer, who were withdrawing their money from whaling to invest in plantations.

Another slump came at the end of the Civil War with a number of plantations going under at the same time. The biggest bankruptcy was that of Walker, Allen & Company. Creditors got less than thirty cents on the dollar.

Planters had realized at the time of the gold rush that they had a real labor problem. It was difficult to find a remedy. The native population did not work out. It was said to be lack of discipline and different attitudes toward labor, or that Hawaiians were lacking in ambition and were not willing to invest time to make money. Yet, this was not quite fair. In ancient times they had built 5,000-acre fishponds and enormous temple platforms.

During the gold rush, hundreds of Hawaiians were going into business for themselves on Maui—growing potatoes and hauling them to the port where they were snapped up and shipped to San Francisco. The Maui fields were called Nu Kaliponi, or New California; potatoes were gold, and a fortune could be dug out of the ground by one man. The potato boom was short-lived, and, when prices dropped, the Hawaiians lost interest. Perhaps the problem was that Hawaiians did not share the white man's concept of time. The real problem was the rapid expansion of the sugar industry at the same time that the Hawaiian population was declining.

The first shipload of Chinese "coolies" was brought to Honolulu in January 1852 and the workers distributed among the planters. After working out their contracts, most of them drifted to the cities to become merchants. These were by no means the first Chinese in Hawai'i. Vancouver had seen one in 1794, and by end of the eighteenth century there were several.

In 1840, on Maui, several Chinese had mules in operation and made sugar on shares. The *Sandwich Island Mirror* for May-June 1840 stated that "the sugar made at Maui is said to be of much better quality than at O'ahu and Kaua'i."

The missionaries helped promote the production of sugar. The Reverend Elias Bond at the north Kohala station on the Big Island was instrumental there in developing the growing of cane. He learned from a Chinese who operated a small sugar mill. Father Bond saw the employment of the natives as a means of saving them from the tragic migrations to Honolulu which were depopulating the country districts of north Kohala.

Dr. Baldwin at Lahaina encouraged the industry, as did many others of the brethren. The Reverend Richard Armstrong wrote from his station at Wailuku, Maui, July 7, 1840: "By a request of the King I have taken some part in inducing the people about me to plant sugar cane. A fine crop of sixty or seventy acres is now on the ground ripe, and a noble water-mill, set up by a China-man, is about going into operation to grind it. I hope some good from this quarter. I keep one plough a going constantly with a view to the support of schools."

Of greater importance than the sugar produced was the effect on the ideas of the people. Sugar growing communities had an air of prosperity and enterprise and both chiefs and commoners benefited, especially the commoners who, as workers, achieved greater independence. A writer in the *Polynesian* June 19, 1841, noted that when the common people "found their time and labor worth something more than hard words and little food, they were not slow in letting their rulers know it. The result has been that they have enjoyed more personal freedom ever since, and their condition has been gradually improving."

In these years other agricultural enterprises included growing of silk worms, coffee, cotton and rice, but none succeeded like sugar. An American farmer grew fifty-five acres of cotton at Haiku, Maui, in 1838, and an enterprising missionary lady, Miss Lydia Brown, taught classes in weaving at Wailuku. Governor Kuakini of Hawai'i visited her school and set up a cotton weaving operation at Kailua-Kona. After his death in 1844, the cotton mill faded out of the picture as did attempts on other islands to produce the cloth.

There were only eleven mills manufacturing sugar and molasses in the islands in 1846; two on Kaua'i, six on Maui, and three on Hawai'i. The following year, by official proclamation, the exclusive ownership of land by the King was finally renounced, and, in 1848, the Great Mahele, or land division of King Kamehameha III provided the final chapter in the collapse of the ancient Hawaiian land system.

In 1851, the use of centrifugals shortened the time for separating the molasses from sugar from weeks to minutes, and the following year one hundred and eighty Chinese contract laborers arrived in Hawai'i on the bark *Thetis*. In 1853, steam power was first introduced in Hawai'i on Maui, replacing water and animal power on many plantations.

In 1854, a Captain Edwards brought a better variety of cane from Tahiti to replace the early plantings made from early cuttings. This was called Lahaina cane because it arrived first at that port. In 1856, Captain James Makee and C. Brewer II bought Hali'imaile Plantation on Maui from the Stephen Reynolds estate for $14,000. This plantation became known as the Brewer Plantation as at that time the firm of C. Brewer and Company became directly interested in sugar.

In 1857, due to labor scarcity, drought, and low prices, the number of plantations dwindled to five, but recovery came quickly and by 1861 there was a large increase in plantations, the number at that time being twenty-two. None of these were using steam as the motive power in grinding, twelve were driven by water, and one by animal power. Sugar tonnage was increasing tremendously as a sugar boom for Hawai'i resulted when the supply from Louisiana was cut off during the Civil War.

In 1862 Wailuku Sugar Company was organized by a syndicate which included C. Brewer and Company manager, Mr. Edward Bailey.

THE VERSATILE MR. BAILEY

Mr. Edward Bailey was a man of many talents. He and his wife arrived in 1837 with the Eighth Company of Missionaries sent out from Boston. They were stationed at Kohala, 1837; Lahainaluna,

1839; and Wailuku Female Seminary, 1840-1848, where they both taught school. Bailey was the architect for, and directed the building of, the old stone church at Wailuku named for Queen Ka-'ahumanu. He designed and built a water-run mill at Wailuku for grinding wheat and sugar and conducted the earliest manufacture of sugar at Wailuku in a venture which later was merged with Wailuku Plantation. He superintended work on the roads and the building of a bridge across the 'Iao Stream, in surveying, and causing to be surveyed native kuleanas (homesteads). He settled land claims, for which he received his principal means of support from the Land Commission. His interest in girls' training schools was shown in the many years he aided in creating and maintaining the Maunaolu Girls' School at Makawao. He was a first rate musician and did much in teaching music. He wrote a synopsis on Hawaiian ferns and a long narrative poem, *Hawai'i Nei: An Idyll*. He drew many of the sketches for the engravings made at Lahainaluna. In his later years he painted delightful landscapes, most of them of scenes on Maui. His paintings are exhibited in the old Bailey House, now a museum in Wailuku.

The Entrepreneurs of Sugar

Activity in the sugar business in central Maui increased rapidly during the 1860s. T. H. Hobron acquired land in Waihe'e for cane cultivation and Captain James Hobron of Makawao purchased the site of the Waihe'e mill. Waikapu Plantation was started by James Louzada and his brother-in-law, William H. Cornwell. A mill was erected at the entrance to Waikapu valley. The Waikapu Plantation changed hands a number of times, finally passing into the control of Wailuku Sugar Company in 1894.

The Lewis mill at Waihee was built by Captain James Hobron. Sam T. Alexander was manager and H. P. Baldwin was head luna (field boss). Both men resigned and established Haiku Plantation on Maui. These two men, brothers-in-law, became the founders of Alexander & Baldwin, which by 1898 had gained controlling interest in Hawaiian Commercial & Sugar Company–the plantation on Maui which was then, and still is, the largest sugar plantation in Hawai'i.

This plantation was originally formed by a remarkable entrepreneur who made a spectacular entry into the field of Hawaiian sugar by buying up most of the sugar crop of the Hawaiian planters in 1876, just at the moment when the Reciprocity Treaty with the United States gave Hawaiian sugar a special advantage in the United States market. The name of this man was Claus Spreckels and his story is a colorful chapter in the history of Hawai'i, and especially of the sugar business on the island of Maui.

THE SUGAR MAGNATE

Claus Spreckels became known as the "Sugar King" of Hawai'i, and the Hawaiian newspapers dubbed him Ona Miliona ("owner of a million"). Spreckels had acquired thousands of acres in the valley of Maui, built two huge ditches to water the dry central plains, and built the most modern and efficient sugar mill perhaps in the world.

Very little remains to remind the residents of Maui of Spreckels himself. Of course, there are the vast fields of cane, the Hawaiian Commercial & Sugar Company (HC&S) which he founded in 1882, and the area where the mill once stood called Spreckelsville.

This is the area of the Maui Country Club, a fine residential section along the north shore just beyond the Kahului airport; but even the post office is gone and residents receive their mail at Paia. Few are aware of the story of Claus Spreckels and his contributions to Maui's development.

The millionaire sugar baron of California arrived in Hawai'i on the steamer *City of San Francisco* on August 24, 1876. The ship also carried the first news of the passage by Congress of the Reciprocity Treaty. A furor was caused as Spreckels at once proceeded to buy up over half of the sugar crop of 1877. Planters in

Hawai'i and San Francisco were bitterly criticized as he had taken advantage of the situation by buying up the sugar before the price rise had had time to take effect.

It was on this first visit that Spreckels became interested in Maui. He studied the situation carefully, and he learned much from the example of Henry P. Baldwin and his partner, S. T. Alexander, who were then making plans for the construction of the Hamakua Ditch. This ditch was the first large engineering project on Maui and was completed just before the lease on the ditch expired on September 30, 1978. The date was of "more than passing concern" to Claus Spreckels, who had purchased a part interest in the Waihee Plantation and now fully grasped the significance of water rights and the importance of the work of the Maui planters.

When Spreckels returned in 1878 to Maui he brought with him an engineer, Hermann Schussler, "and set in motion the first of a series of enterprises that for many years made him the most powerful figure in Hawai'i's economic structure–a powerful factor also in the political life of the kingdom."

Spreckels continued to study the potential of central Maui for sugar production, cultivated his friendship with King Ka-lakaua, and, through the King, secured purchase and lease of some 40,000 acres of Maui land. He applied for and received water rights for the northern slope of Haleakala and the right to conduct the water to his lands on the isthmus of Maui by means of a ditch. He then developed the great Maui plantation and mill and organized under the name of the Hawaiian Commercial & Sugar Company.

"The first Spreckels ditch ran from the northern slopes to the central plans, some thirty miles of ditch, tunnels, pipes, flumes and trestles. It crossed thirty gulches, some 2,000 feet wide and 400 feet deep. Twenty-eight tunnels, 3 x 8 feet, some of them 500 feet long, had been cut through solid rock. Twenty-one thousand feet of pipe had been used. The ditch itself was 8 feet wide by 5 feet deep, with a fall of about 3 feet in a mile. It delivered up to 60 cubic feet of water a second. All this involved an outlay of about $500,000."

Nevertheless, there can be no doubt that the earlier Hamakua Ditch of Alexander and Baldwin was the greater achievement when it is considered that neither of these men had had any formal engineering training, nor did they have the services of a Hermann Schussler. It was much more difficult for them to raise $80,000, the cost of the Hamakua Ditch, than it was for Spreckels to raise half a million. The Hamakua Ditch was shorter, running seventeen miles mauka (on the mountain side) of the Spreckels ditch, and delivered about 40,000,000 gallons of water a day as compared to 60,000,000 gallons a day delivered by the larger ditch. The story of the building of the Hamakua Ditch is an exciting one and is the more familiar to Mauians. It is told in a later section of this chapter.

As the cane fields spread over the Wailuku and Waikapu commons, the thirsty land cried out for more water than could be supplied by the ditch from northeastern Maui. In 1882, therefore, Spreckels made an agreement with the Waihee Sugar Company by which he obtained, for a rental of $10,000 a year, a large part of the water supply controlled by that company. A ditch was dug to carry this water to the HC&S fields on the western side of the Maui isthmus. Thus, in the course of a few years, the life and appearance of central Maui were transformed.

MONEY AND POLITICS

Claus Spreckels was a controversial figure cast, as he was, in the mold of the nineteenth-century robber barons who established great fortunes before the turn of the century in America's industrial revolution. He was a crony of King Ka-lakaua and was able at one time to persuade the King to dismiss a cabinet which held up the granting of the water rights on Maui ardently sought by Spreckels. On this account, he loaned the King the sum of $40,000.

He also bought from the Princess Ruth Ke-eli-kolani her purported claim to one half of the crown lands of Hawai'i for the sum of $10,000. He had no intention of claiming one half of all the royal lands but used his claim as a bargaining tool to get control in fee simple of the Wailuku Commons, which were part of the crown lands he had leased for the plantation.

THE MARVELOUS MILL

Many distinguished visitors came to Maui to see the wonderful mill at Spreckelsville, and members of the royal family visited at various times. These included the King, Princess Ruth, and Dowager Queen Emma. Everyone was intrigued with the marvel of the electric lights which Spreckels had installed in the mill.

Queen Emma described one of these visits in a letter to a friend: "Last night Mr. J. D. Spreckels (the son) called and invited me to go and see the electric light which they use at the mill, so this evening was started by train with a party of nearly 600 people for Pu'unene [the mill was actually a mile or so seawards of the present Pu'unene mill] where his mill stands. Everything is carried on on the most extensive scale, and the newest inventions are used of machinery, etc. Mr. Spreckels showed us the electric machines where electricity is made and conducted through wires to every part of the mill. You have seen the light no doubt, so can fancy how like unto day was the entire interior and exterior of [the] building. It really was wonderfully grand…There was music, vocal and instrumental, wine and cake at his house and music in [the] train."

CONTRIBUTIONS OF SPRECKELS

Jacob Adler, his biographer, believes that the positive contributions of Claus Spreckels to Hawai'i, and especially Maui, tend to be overshadowed by his reputation for rascality. Though this is not entirely undeserved, the positive contributions remain more significant, more lasting, and of benefit to the Islands' economy and people.

In the 1880s, Spreckels' investment in the islands amounted to well over $4,000,000. "Maui owed much of its wealth to his enterprise and example." The arrivals and departures of his Oceanic Steamship Lines ships contributed to the development of the Kahului harbor, the shipping point for the sugar from the Maui plantations.

Some other "firsts" which Spreckels brought to the sugar industry were the five-roller mill, railroad hauling of cane, controlled irrigation, and use of the steam plow, first used by Spreckels' plantation for more effective plowing to reduce use of manpower and increase the sugar yield.

In 1898 at the annual meeting of HC&S, control of "the magnificent plantation" slipped from Claus Spreckels' grasp and that of his sons, Gus and Rudolph. J. B. Castle and Associates, with H. P. Baldwin and S. T. Alexander, took control.

Claus Spreckels was seventy years old, and his years of greatest power in Hawai'i (1876-1886) were over. He made one last attempt at a political comeback just after the Revolution of 1893, when he tried to restore Queen Lili'uokalani to the throne. He continued to be a power on the mainland in sugar and other industries until his death in 1908.

The Maui Dynasty of Sugar

The growing of cane and its production into sugar attracted two enterprising missionary sons who became the partners and founders of the company named for them, Alexander & Baldwin. This company today is far and away the biggest private land owner on the island of Maui.

Samuel T. Alexander and Henry Perrine Baldwin, lifelong friends and business partners, were also brothers-in-law. Sam Alexander's sister, Emily, became Mrs. H. P. Baldwin, and these two became the progenitors of a new kind of Maui dynasty, the Maui dynasty of sugar.

Henry Perrine Baldwin, who "succeeded" Claus Spreckels as "Sugar King" of Maui, was an altogether different sort of man. Although they might be compared in terms of managerial and organizational skill and foresighted business acumen, the resemblance would end there.

Baldwin, still referred to on Maui many years after his death as "H. P.," was the son of the medical missionary who came to Hawai'i with the Fourth Company in 1830. He was born at Lahaina in 1842, and it was at Lahaina where the Alexander and Baldwin families became close friends.

Considered one of the greatest explorers ever, Captain James Cook (1728-1779) was the first Westerner to discover the Hawaiian Islands, changing dramatically the course of Hawaiian history. On his second visit to the Islands he was killed in an altercation at Kealakekua on the Island of Hawai'i, perhaps having overstayed his welcome. **(Hawai'i State Archives)**

Raised during long years of peace, Liholiho succeeded his father, Kamehameha I, at age twenty-two with neither military nor ruling experience, sharing his power with Ka'ahumanu, his father's politically influential widow. Pressured by Ka'ahumanu, Liholiho ordered the destruction of heiau and religious idols in 1819, thereby ending the chiefly state religion and the kapu system. **(Hawai'i State Archives)** / Ka'ahumanu was the heiress of the Maui royal dynasty and favorite wife of Kamehameha I, who had unified the Hawaiian Islands. Originally she rejected Christianity, but in 1825 a near fatal illness followed by recovery led to her conversion—a spiritual transformation that had important consequences. **(Hawai'i State Archives)**

Ships of a French expedition reached Maui in 1786 led by Admiral Jean François de Galaup, comte de La Pérouse (1741-1788). The most celebrated French navigator of the eighteenth century, his crews were the first Westerners to go ashore on Maui at a spot now called La Pérouse Bay. **(Hawai'i State Archives)**

Rev. Dwight Baldwin and his wife, Charlotte Fowler, arrived with the Fourth Company of American missionaries in 1831. After a brief stay at Waimea, Island of Hawai'i, they served from 1835 to 1870 at Lahaina. During all those years he was not only a pastor but a busy physician as well. He also translated into Hawaiian a new edition of the first five books of the Bible. **(Hawai'i State Archives)** / In 1843, the second Hawaiian licensed to preach by the missionaries was David Malo, a graduate of Lahainaluna School, and later the author of a brilliant collection of oral histories published as *Hawaiian Antiquities*. Originally a friend and outspoken defender of the missionaries, Malo was not ordained until 1852. This perhaps contributed to his later growing anti-foreign sentiments which culminated in his desire to be buried high above Lahaina, far from the rising tide of foreigners. **(Hawai'i State Archives)**

As the sandalwood trade waned, whaling became Hawai'i's economic mainstay. Each season the crews of the American whaling fleets descended like locusts upon Lahaina, seeking provisions and the sailors' traditional pleasures of the bottle and the flesh. **(Hawai'i State Archives)** / To promote higher education among Christianized Hawaiian men, the Lahainaluna Mission Seminary was established on Maui in 1831. The first class of twenty-five was trained to become schoolteachers and eventually preachers of the Gospel. The school's engraver, Kepohoni, who worked at its printing shop, made this view of the seminary in the 1840s. **(Hawai'i State Archives)**

Wailuku Plantation (1875) with Ī'ao Valley to the rear was the site of Wailuku Sugar Company, formed in 1862 by a group of partners including C. Brewer and Company, Ltd., and managed by Rev. Edward Bailey. By 1867, it was producing 800 tons of sugar from 500 acres of cane. **(Baker-Van Dyke Collection)**

The growth of the sugar industry on Maui acted as a catalyst for the development of towns like Wailuku, which was becoming the island's commercial center when this photograph was taken in 1905. A new courthouse opened in 1907, making Wailuku the island's governmental headquarters as well. **(Hawai'i State Archives)**

The nearby town of Kahului also thrived during the reign of "King Sugar" because its harbor was a central location for shipping. This photograph was taken between 1903 and 1905 from the freight depot of the Kahului Railroad, which regularly transported tons of harvested sugar to the docks. **(Bishop Museum)**

The town of Spreckelsville was named after "Sugar King" Claus Spreckels. This photo was taken at his departure from Hawai'i in 1898. During his 20 years in the Islands he contributed much to the development of the sugar industry, although he was a controversial, robber-baron figure. **(Hawai'i State Archives)** / Wailuku Sugar Mill at a later date. **(Hawai'i State Archives)**

Puʻunēnē Mill was considered the largest sugar mill in the world when it was photographed in 1912. Operated for over forty years by the Hawaiian Commercial and Sugar Company under the direction of missionary descendant Henry P. Baldwin, and later under his son, Frank Baldwin, the Puʻunēnē plantation possessed 33,000 acres of fertile Maui lands by 1935. A large multi-ethnic labor force kept 16,000 acres of these lands under sugarcane cultivation as Puʻunēnē town grew to a population of close to 10,000 people. **(Hawaiʻi State Archives)**

With the stabilization of immigrant families and the birth of the second generation, a culturally diverse society emerged in Hawai'i. In 1915, these
Portuguese families from Lahaina, Maui reflected the European influences
that contributed to the multi-ethnic mix of both plantation and island life.
Plantation workers cottage, Lahaina, Maui, 1910. **(Bishop Museum)**

Armine von Tempski and her favorite colt, 1908. Encouraged by Jack London to be a writer, her *Born in Paradise* (1904) tells of growing up in the ranch lands of Haleakalā where her father was manager of the 60,000 acre Haleakalā Ranch. **(Baker-Van Dyke Collection)**

Built in 1912, the Wo Hing Society and Social Hall served Maui's local Chinese community. An altar room on the second floor was used for religious services. Beginning in the 1940s, as many of Maui's Chinese pursued new business opportunities in Honolulu, the building fell into disrepair. It was restored in the mid-1980s by the Lahaina Restoration Foundation and is now open to the public as the Wo Hing Museum. **(Hawai'i State Archives)**

SHORE LEAVE U.S.NAVY
1940 LAHAINA, MAUI

Lahaina's older reputation as a whaling port faded into the past as Front Street hummed with traffic in the 1920s. By the 1930s, Lahaina had a population of 7,000, most of whom worked for West Maui sugar and pineapple operations. / Preceding and during World War II, Lahaina hosted ships and sailors of the US Navy who put ashore in small boats that tied up at Māla Wharf. **(Nakamoto Art Studio)**

Despite a heavy military influx, Mauians were grateful for the sacrifices of the young soldiers and sailors stationed or visiting the island during World War II. Local hula dancers and musicians would frequently entertain U.S. military personnel. **(Nakamoto Art Studio)**

Kaho'olawe, once used as a landing by Hawaiian fishermen, became a ranch in 1858. During the second half of the twentieth century it was used by the US military for war exercises and bombing target practice. In 1994, the Federal government bowed to decades of protest and returned control of the island to the Hawaiian people. **(Mutual Publishing)** / Once exclusively pineapple fields, Kapalua on Maui's north-west coast now houses a resort complex surrounding three of Maui's best beaches. Pineapple was originally grown in areas unsuitable for sugar. **(USDA Soil Conservation Service)**

As the family grew, so grew the powerful control of sugar lands and related industry. At the same time, the political power of the heads of the companies also grew strong.

Baldwin was the most important man on Maui during three, perhaps four, decades from 1870 to his death in 1911. He and Alexander saw the possibilities in sugar which could be achieved in Mauiís dry central plains only if large quantities of water were available to irrigate the cane. Together they built the Hamakua ditch and brought the water in quantity from the rainy windward slopes of Haleakala to irrigate their East Maui fields.

THE MALIKO GULCH

Sam Alexander, speaking of their plans for the Hamakua Ditch, wrote: "The Maliko gulch...is by far the most formidable gulch we will have to contend with. It is 300 feet deep and 800 feet broad and the sides precipitous and consisting of solid rock. I propose to pipe the water across the gulch. Have a pipe made of boiler iron and riveted about eighteen inches in diameter, which ought to be, I suppose, about 1/10 inches thick at the top of the gulch and increase in thickness up to 3/10 inches at the bottom of the gulch. This pipe I would propose to dub well with hot tar and pitch. The length of the pipe which I propose to put across the Maliko gulch will be just 1,100 feet."

Sam Alexander planned the historic ditch in all its details; Baldwin completed it, demonstrating immense personal courage along the way. In March, 1876, only a few months before, H. P. lost his right arm in an accident at his mill near Paia. Showing an associate the uneven gap between the rollers which crush the cane, he put his right hand through the opening. The machinery was still turned on and before the gears could be reversed, his arm was caught and crushed to the elbow.

H. P. took a stiff shot of brandy and coolly sent a rider miles down the mountain to fetch a doctor. The horse died from the exertion; Baldwin's arm was amputated at the shoulder that afternoon, and he almost immediately began learning to eat, write, and even play the organ at the Makawao Church with his left hand. Soon he went back to work even harder on the plantation and especially on the new ditch.

The problem of crossing the Maliko gulch was further complicated by the refusal of the workers to lower themselves over the cliff and into the deep ravine. H. P. again demonstrated his courage. Clutching a rope with his legs and one arm, he swung 300 feet down into the gulch. The workers, shamed, followed his example. He is said to have repeated his demonstration each day until the gulch had been spanned.

H. P. Baldwin became active in politics and was elected to the Legislature of the Hawai'i Territory in 1887. He belonged to the Reform Party ("Damned Missionaries") which favored constitutional monarchy. The great *luau* that H. P. gave in honor of Queen Lili'uokalani in the *kukui* grove in 'Iao Valley was long remembered.

During the stormy years before and after the queen was dethroned in 1893, Baldwin was a great reconciler of the various factions, trusted by Hawaiian and haole alike. A loyal citizen of the Hawaiian Kingdom, he accepted the overthrow reluctantly, but bowed to the inevitable and switched to the Republic. When the United States annexed Hawai'i in 1898, H. P. threw a huge *luau*. The annexation was delayed by twenty-four hours, but, as news travelled slowly in that day, he was ahead of schedule by twenty-four hours so that it was after the party that his guests learned that they had been the very first to celebrate!

H. P. Baldwin was a religious man and was recognized for his integrity. Once he prayed for rain to save his first plantation, promising to give of every earning some portion to the Lord's work. It rained, and H. P. kept his promise. He became very rich and his benefactions were numerous, though most often done quietly and without publicity. He rebuilt the old church at Lahaina and contributed to other churches. He built schools on Maui, donating a large building fully furnished at his own expense to Maunaolu Seminary. He bulk a dormitory for young boys at the Hansen's disease colony at Kalaupapa on Moloka'i. He died at Makawao, still president of A & B, at sixty-eight.

SUGAR AND LAND

Alexander & Baldwin's history has been one of solid growth. The original 11.94 acres purchased for $110 in 1869 by two hard-working missionary offspring grew into a corporation with $1.5 billion in assets.

By the end of 1999, A&B's Hawaiian Commercial & Sugar Co. was the last remaining sugar plantation on Maui, and one of only two left in the islands. The plantation survived while others failed because of its fertile lands and focus on improving agricultural practices, resulting in high yields and low production costs.

Despite substantial challenges in sugar and in its coffee-growing on Kaua'i, A&B had evolved into a diversified corporation whose other businesses made it profitable.

Ocean transportation through its Matson Navigation Co. subsidiary was an important part of these assets. The corporation's principal business, however, had become property management and development. It owned more than 90,000 acres in Hawai'i and commercial properties in six western states. On Maui, the company owned 69,050 acres in 1999, with 52,700 acres in various agricultural uses.

A&B first became involved in planned development with the founding of "Dream City," a residential community started in 1949. Building a model town on Maui was a dream of the brothers Frank F. and Harry Baldwin, sons of H. P. Baldwin. They wanted their employees to have an opportunity to own attractive, reasonably priced homes. At the same time, the plantations needed to close down aging and dilapidated "camps" where employees lived near the sugar fields. Substandard housing had been a key issue in the Territory-wide 1946 sugar strike.

The new town would include clean, modern three-bedroom houses on 10,000-square-foot lots, along with schools, churches, parks and Maui's first shopping mall, the Kahului Shopping Center. Dream City was an instant success as buyers lined up to buy a house-and-lot package for as little as $6,600. Development of Kahului continued into the 1980s. By that time A&B Properties Inc. had sold 3,000 lots in Kahului.

By century's end, the simple houses of the original Dream City were selling for more than $200,000.

One unanticipated effect of the growth of Kahului was that Wailuku, for decades the commercial center of Maui, languished as first the Maui Mall and then the Kaahumanu Center opened, drawing retail business down the hill. Wailuku's decline appeared to be reversing as antique and boutique-style shops filled its vintage buildings in the late 1990s.

PINEAPPLE

Pineapple became an important crop in Hawai'i, and flourished in the sunny plantations of Maui. The Baldwins discovered this while developing their great sugar lands on the island. A company called Baldwin Packers was acquired by H. P. along with its lands at Kapalua on the northwest coast of Maui. Baldwin Packers eventually became Maui Pineapple Company, the largest producer of pineapple on Maui. Its development was watched over carefully by J. Walter Cameron who had married Frances Baldwin, granddaughter of H. P. Taking over Maui Pineapple, of which A & B owned controlling interest, he led the Maui company as it developed over the 1950s and 1960s. On his father's retirement, Colin C. Cameron became manager for A & B, then resigned from Maui Pineapple as a struggle for its control ensued. In a surprise move, a multimillion dollar deal in which the Camerons traded A & B stock and cash for controlling stock in the pineapple company, the Camerons won control. Colin became president, the name was changed to Maui Land & Pineapple Company, and the management began the development of an elaborate resort complex at Kapalua.

Colin Cameron died suddenly in 1992. Members of the Cameron family retained control of the pineapple operation, Kapalua Land Co. and commercial property development such as that of Kaahumanu Center in Kahului. Like the sugar industry, pineapple faced challenges due to competition from areas of the world where production costs were lower. Pineapple fought back in part by focusing on fresh fruit products.

In 1999, America Online chief Stephen M. Case purchased 41.2 percent of the company's common stock, previously owned by the late Harry Weinberg. This was the latest development in a relationship between two families that dated back a century, to the days when Steve Case's great-grandfather, Judge D. H. Case, was an associate and business partner of H. P. Baldwin.

SUGAR AND AGRICULTURE

Sugar has been grown and processed nearly everywhere on Maui. Hana, at the eastern end, was once a prosperous plantation and mill, as was Kipahulu beyond Hana. Sugar was grown high above Makena at Ulupalakua. There once was a mill at Olowalu, and ruins of abandoned sugar mills are found at all these places. At Hamakuapoko the high stone walls of the ruined mill are only held up by the aerial roots of the banyan trees which have split the old mill apart.

Of the many plantations once flourishing on Maui, just one remained at the end of the twentieth century. Hawaiian Commercial & Sugar Co. still maintained thousands of acres of sugar in the central plain, though its Paia Mill closed in 1999, leaving only the Pu'unene Mill in operation. In 2001, only HC&S and the Gay & Robinson plantation on Kaua'i continued to produce sugar in Hawai'i.

HC&S struggled with drought and with competition for the water carried to Central Maui by the ditch system its founders built. Newcomers whose family history had not evolved out of the sugar plantations were particularly likely to complain about the inconvenience and possible health hazards of smoke from the burning required by the plantation's system of harvest. The plantation continued to research both new ways to harvest and new ways to use its crop.

Other Maui plantations have lost the fight to survive, victims of market forces that made it cheaper to produce sugar abroad or from beets or corn.

In the 1980s, Wailuku Agribusiness Co., formerly known as Wailuku Sugar Co., moved from farming sugar to growing pineapple and macadamia nuts. Those crops were in turn phased out, and small parcels of the company land were leased to independent farmers.

In 1999, after 139 years, Pioneer Mill Inc. concluded its final sugar harvest. Its death left the green hills above Lahaina brown and dusty, with an uncertain future ahead.

Diversified agriculture continued to play a part, though a small one, in Maui's economy. In Kula, farmers found success with crops such as potatoes, onions, carnations and the exotic protea flower. Coffee grew on some of the Pioneer Mill land above Ka'anapali. In Hana, farmers produced a variety of tropical flowers.

Though Maui's benevolent climate seemed ideal for agriculture, the high costs of land, water, labor and imported equipment made economic success difficult. Critics pointed out that pineapple required pesticides, and sugar used large amounts of water, not to mention the irritation of cane smoke. But no easy answers presented themselves, even after generations of agriculturists had tried everything from rice to rubber to silk worms in search of alternative crops that could be grown on a large scale.

CHAPTER 9

FROM MANY LANDS: NEW PEOPLES

*It seemed that the population problem as well as
the labor problem, could only be solved by immigration
from abroad, either voluntary or assisted.*

– Kuykendall, *The Hawaiian Kingdom.*

Two factors which affected the population, and along with it the labor problem in the islands, were the continuous decrease in the native Hawaiian population and the growth of agricultural enterprises described in the previous chapter. Hawai'i's total population probably reached its lowest point about 1875 but began its long upward climb several years later, as shown by the census of 1878. But the Hawaiian and part-Hawaiian segment of the population did not reach its lowest point until long after 1878.

Statistics of those years show that far from being unsuited to plantation labor, or considered inefficient workers, Hawaiian labor was considered the best obtainable by many planters. As late as 1869 some plantations employed Hawaiian labor exclusively. Kuykendall quotes from several sources, one of whom commented in the 1870 report of the Hawaiian Immigration Society as follows: "Whilst the population has largely diminished, there are probably as many or more Hawaiians working on plantations today than ever before, and doing it cheerfully of their own free will…The true reason why there is a dearth of Hawaiian labor is the increase of the planting interests from some 2,000,000 of pounds in nine or ten years to 18 or 20,000,000, requiring from eight to ten times as many men now as then; also the additional fact that more Hawaiian seamen are employed now than then…" This source found more Hawaiians employed in such labor than ever before, and statistics for that year (1873) showed that out of 3,786 laborers employed on thirty-five plantations, 2,627 were Hawaiian men and 364 were Hawaiian women. "The Hawaiian men thus employed were more than 50 percent of the able-bodied native male population of the Kingdom."

Nevertheless, the population decline was palpable and became a matter of public concern of the kings and their advisers, of the Hawaiian legislature, and of the sugar planters. There was continuous public debate and various plans were put forward in the 1860s and 1870s. Out of the numerous proposals, immigration of labor from China and Japan to fill the population and labor gap seemed to many to be the most feasible plan, and it was from these two countries that the largest contingents of immigrants came, though supplemented by Caucasians, including Portuguese, and Filipinos, Koreans, Puerto Ricans, Germans, Pacific Islanders and many others.

"What may be called the 'reciprocity period' [1876-1900] witnessed a remarkable change in the size and character of the population of the Hawaiian Islands."

In that period the population rose from 55,500 in 1876 to 154,000 in 1900. The following table shows the changes in percentages:

	1876	*1900*
Hawaiian & Part-Hawaiian	89.2%	26.0%
Caucasian	6.3	17.5
Oriental	4.5	56.5
	100.0%	*100.0%*

This chapter contains the stories of several families who came from distant lands in the nineteenth and early twentieth centuries to work on the sugar plantations of Maui. Perhaps through the eyes of these people, some insight into the lives of the immigrants may be gained.

THE CHINESE

It is believed that the first Chinese to see Hawaiʻi were the fifty carpenters and smiths from Canton who accompanied Captain John Meares to Nootka Sound on the American northwest coast. In 1788 Meares' ships, the *Felice* and *Iphigenia*, were in Hawaiian waters with the small schooner *North West American*, which the Chinese artisans had built for him at Nootka Sound. The *Iphigenia* and *North West American* wintered for four months in the islands and while there Kamehameha visited the ships and requested that two of the Chinese carpenters be left with him to build for him a schooner similar to the *North West American*. This was refused although Chinese carpenters, again at the King's request, did build a mounting for a swivel gun which they attached to one of Kamehameha's double canoes.

In 1789, Captain Simon Metcalf had a crew aboard the *Eleanora* which included forty-five Chinese, one of whom may have gone ashore after the massacre on Maui with John Young at Kealakekua Bay. If that were the case he would have been detained with Young by Kamehameha and thus could have been the "one Chinaman" noted among eleven foreigners in Kamehameha's retinue by Vancouver five years later.

Although a number of very successful Chinese sugar masters and merchants were well established in Hawaiʻi in the first half of the nineteenth century, the first contract field laborers arrived on Maui from Hong Kong in 1852. There were one hundred and seventy-five men, mostly Hakka from Kwangtung Province. They came on five-year contracts to the sugar plantations. Their pay was $3 a month plus passage, room and board. They were a hardy people who had survived great hardship in China, and they were looking for a better life for themselves and their families. Other waves arrived in the next few decades, particularly in the 1890s, most of whom intended to return to China, but many stayed on.

"UNCLE SHINN"

Among the Chinese who arrived on Maui was a fifteen-year-old boy named Shing Sam Shin. He was one of a number of Chinese who worked as farm labor in upland Maui at Kula on land leased from the Crown. Shing Sam Shin worked hard and saved up enough money to send to China for a bride, Liu Moi. A son was born whom they named Ten Sung Shinn.

T. S. Shinn, known to thousands of Maui Boy Scouts and friends as "Uncle Shinn," elected to stay on Maui when his parents decided to return. His story is one of hard work and a successful career and life. Though Uncle Shinn's career was more successful than most, his life, especially his early life, as he told it with gusto, was typical of many of the Chinese who became such an important part of the multiracial society of Hawai'i.

"Like all Chinese, my father came to Maui to better himself. When they arrived all they had were the shirts on their backs. My father's people had been farmers in Hong Kong. We grew our own food and sent money to poor relatives in Hong Kong."

"It was really hard. I never wore shoes until I was about ten years old. We were sort of hardy stock." The land was hard to work and the rains were not dependable. Drought conditions were common. But the Chinese who lived and worked around Keokea enjoyed the healthiest climate to be found almost anywhere; they also enjoyed themselves and became good friends and neighbors of the Hawaiians living there.

Approximately eighty Chinese families moved to Kula between 1880 and 1910. By 1900, there were approximately 700 Chinese living there. For a period of thirty to forty years Kula supported a thriving community which included English and Chinese schools, Christian churches, a Hung Men Society, gambling joints and opium dens, general stores, and dozens of operating farms and cattle ranches.

"In those days we all had oxens. It took a full day to go from Kula to Kahului." Until he was grown Shinn worked on the farm, went to school and, after school, "we had to chase the chickens out of the corn."

Once he had graduated from Keokea, Shinn had to leave Kula for further education. He moved in with a relative in Paia whence he could take the train each day to Wailuku, where he enrolled in St. Anthony's School, at that time noted for turning out businessmen. One of his teachers at St. Anthony's was Manuel, the father of Mayor Elmer Cravalho. He then went to work for the Kahului Railroad Co., at the same time helping out as a translator for Ah Fook, who founded the supermarket by that name in Kahului in 1917.

In 1923 Shinn went to work for a company which became MDG Supply. In 1978, though "semi-retired" at 78, T. S. Shinn was still vice president, treasurer and secretary of MDG Supply and still involved in many a charitable enterprise on Maui and, indeed, in Hong Kong and elsewhere. He once said that "a lot of the big businessmen in Honolulu are Maui boys. One reason they didn't stay was because they weren't allowed to own land here. It was easier to get a farm on Oʻahu."

"Uncle Shinn's" parents, like so many of the original Chinese immigrants, returned to China. Their children stayed. When he was asked about the hard work in his younger years, he said: "I enjoyed my work. My attitude is 'where there is love, there is no burden.'" It is an attitude that well served T. S. Shinn and many others of Chinese ancestry who, in turn, served the community of Maui.

T. S. Shinn died in 1980. The Maui Chamber of Commerce annually honors his memory with an award given to a citizen who has made substantial contributions to the community.

SUN YAT-SEN ON MAUI

It is an interesting yet little-known fact that the "Father of the Chinese Revolution" was a frequent visitor to the village of Kula, Maui in the 1880s. His older brother, Sun Ah Mi, was a prominent rancher there, having leased or bought some eight hundred acres of land and five hundred head of cattle. He was the only coffee planter in the area.

Sun Yat-sen first visited the Islands in 1879 and graduated from Iolani School in Honolulu in 1882 at the age of sixteen. He returned to China to study medicine but, after several years, journeyed again to Hawai'i to seek support for the revolution. For their safety, Dr. Sun moved his wife and family to Maui where they lived with Sun Mi and his family.

Sun Mi had obtained for his brother a false birth certificate which gave his birthplace as O'ahu and his domicile as "Kula, island of Maui," where he was listed as a physician. This enabled the Chinese revolutionary leader to travel more freely in the United States and, as a United States citizen, to be free of harassment by the Manchus.

Historians differ as to the support which Sun Yat-sen obtained from the Chinese in Hawai'i. Some say that the revolution received minimal and inconsistent support while others argue that Hawai'i was the mainstay of overseas support for the Chinese revolution and that thousands of dollars were donated to the cause by the Chinese in Hawai'i.

The site of the Sun Mi ranch is known, but the ranch house and buildings are long since gone. Sun Yat-sen made many visits there in the early years of this century and whenever visiting Kula was consulted for medical advice. In 1975 a lady who lives in Wailuku, Mrs. Pak Hoy Wong, recalled that she received a vaccination by Dr. Sun, administered with a bamboo needle.

"Mrs. Sun Yat-sen and Mrs. Sun Mi became regular guests of the Rev. and Mrs. Chong How Fo every Christmas: 'They came to Kula on horseback, a Hawaiian lad with them. They had bound feet, you see ...Christmas Eve they came...They spent one night with us every Christmas for eight or nine years. After that they moved to Kahului for a little while. It was too far for them to come...'

"When word reached Kula that the 1912 revolution was a success, the town broke out in celebration. China had taken a giant and historic step forward, and Dr. Sun Yat-sen, a familiar and respected personality in Kula, had become the Republic's first leader."

After 1911, some of the Chinese farmers in Kula were able to buy their lands, but before this arrangement was concluded, a number of Kula farmers saw their land divided into homesteads and leased to others. These farmers were forced to move elsewhere in the islands.

Then, in 1918, some forty families left Kula because their farms were sold to a wealthy rancher. The leases to the land had not expired, but the farmers were unaware of their right to challenge the eviction.

"The families who managed to remain in Kula continued to farm the land and engage in community activities, but for various reasons, family after family departed Kula and the Chinese community never re-attained the level of bustling activity it had enjoyed in the early 1900's.

"Among the reasons which had prompted the exodus of many Kula families during the 1910's and 20's were: severe drought which ruined crops and killed livestock, soil which was reaching depletion level after years of harvesting and tilling, lack of educational opportunities for their children, and loss of land due to parceling of homesteads.

"Most of these people moved to Honolulu, where the day was not as endless and the opportunities were more varied. Others moved to Haiku or other parts of Maui or to other islands."

THE PORTUGUESE

In the Peabody Museum of Salem, Massachusetts, there is found the logbook of a whale ship named the *Massachusetts*. It is an interesting document in Maui history as that ship visited Maui in 1791, and the log contains a complete description of the Olowalu Massacre with some details not observed in other accounts.

One detail of this sort is the naming of the Portuguese seaman* whose murder led to the terrible massacre. The log gives his name as Antony. He was assigned to guard the cutter of the *Eleanora* the night she was stolen by Hawaiians off the village at La Pérouse Bay. He cried out in alarm and was killed. Some of his bones were later returned to Captain Metcalf with the keel of the cutter.

---

* Other accounts have described the sailor as "a Manila man."

The unfortunate Antony may have been the first Portuguese to visit Maui. Many more were to follow on the whale ships, so many of which carried Portuguese seamen from the Azores. These islands in the Atlantic were one of the whaling grounds in the nineteenth century and whale ships of British and American ownership often recruited able seamen there, some of them experienced whalemen.

But it was not until the 1890s that Portuguese in any significant numbers came to Hawai'i. They were brought in as much to strengthen the declining population as they were to labor in the fields, and the great difference between Portuguese immigration and the Chinese and Japanese was that a large percentage brought their wives and families, thus clearly intending to stay.

Bringing immigrants from the Azores was a more expensive procedure than in the cases of the Asian immigrants who had come earlier. The contracts were usually for three years, not counting the time spent aboard ship (about six months).

An unmarried man was paid $16 a month for ten hours work a day in the field; twelve hours a day in the sugar house. They were furnished with houses, bedding and medical attention. A married man with one child was paid $18 a month; a man with more than one child was paid $20.

Portuguese (17,500 were recruited between 1878 and 1887 from the Azores and Madeira Islands) were regarded by the planters as a desirable supplement to the Chinese laborers and by the government as effective rebuilders of the declining Hawaiian population. Approximately one quarter of the total immigration of Portuguese occurred between 1906 and 1913, although a considerable number of them were later lost to California.

Although the total number of Chinese imported to Hawai'i was more than twice that of Portuguese, by 1910 the Portuguese population had exceeded the Chinese.

Although the Portuguese on Maui are engaged in every type of business and industry, and in every part of the island, perhaps the most recognizable group are those living in Maui's so-called Upcountry where ranching and farming are the principal occupations. Portuguese residents there center their activities around the ranching town of Makawao, its Catholic St. Joseph's Church, and at Kula which is the location of the beautiful octagonal church whose altar was brought from Portugal itself.

Although large numbers of Portuguese have merged with people of other racial groups, in the post World War II period there has been a renaissance of ethnic pride and a revival of the ancient culture which their ancestors knew in the homeland.

Alfred "Flako" Boteilho

Among the Portuguese arriving in Hawai'i in the 1890s was a young couple who brought with them their two children—one born on the ship during a six-month voyage from the Azores. They were Mariano Boteilho and his wife, Antonia. Like those who accompanied them, they were brought to Hawai'i by the Hawaiian Sugar Planters Association. An H.S.P.A. agent met them at Honolulu and, assigning them to Maui, handed each man $10, a loan that was to be repaid at the rate of $1 a month. Mariano was assigned to the HC&S plantation where he worked in the fields, becoming a luna, or supervisor, in 1910. Like many other men from the Azores, he stayed with the plantation after his contract was fulfilled, although it was possible to leave.

Mariano and Antonia were the parents of Alfred "Flako" Boteilho, who, after a lifetime of working on the plantation, retired to Paia in 1975. In a retrospective interview which appeared in the Mayor's Bicentennial Report (1976), "Flako" and his wife, Laura, recalled those early days of life growing up and working on a Maui plantation.

"My father and the others cleared the land for the first fields with their hands," Boteilho said with a fierce pride that continues to mark Maui's descendants of those early immigrants. In those days most of Maui's population lived in plantation camps that were set up along ethnic lines. Each group of workers, including the less numerous Koreans, Puerto Ricans, and Spaniards, had its own camp or section of a camp.

Although mostly living separately, the various ethnic groups all worked together. Their commonality was the hot sun and the straining backs in the fields. It was a commonality that bridged language, cultural, and religious differences. It was a commonality that formed the sinews of Maui life.

Life in the camps for the Portuguese began when they first arrived. The houses were built and ready. At first there was only an oven for every five families. Later, individual families built their own ovens for baking the delicious round loaves of Portuguese bread so popular on Maui.

Mrs. Alfred Boteilho (Laura) pointed out that "you could save money if you raised your own food and were careful." The money saved was often used to buy a small plot of land in the Upcountry area that reminded the immigrants of their homeland. The company houses prepared for Portuguese occupation each had its own altar, and priests were on hand to greet the new arrivals. "Most of the Portuguese went straight from the boat to the church," Laura said. She added that, "A big reason the Portuguese came to Hawai'i was because the children were promised schooling."

Work, the church, and the family. These were the centers of the Portuguese life on the plantation. That and pride, a pride that extended to the plantation itself.

"I feel that without sugar and agriculture, Hawai'i would not be as progressive as it is. As far as I'm concerned, life on the plantation has been good to me…The fact is I am employed by the best plantation in Hawai'i and life has been beautiful," Boteilho said in an article printed after he had worked for the plantation for forty-eight years. Alfred Boteilho died in 1979. The county gym in Paia was named in his honor.

THE JAPANESE

The story of Japanese immigration parallels that of the Portuguese in some respects, including the expectation that they would serve to revive the "dying native population." First, efforts to import Japanese laborers were made in 1868. The Japanese government did not approve, and only 148 persons of an expected 350 left the country for Hawaiʻi. No further immigration occurred until 1885 when Japanese peasants, largely from the southern prefectures, began arriving in large numbers for plantation work. By 1900, the census listed 61,111 Japanese living in Hawaiʻi. The planters seemed well pleased with these industrious and thrifty workers, but their cordiality and that of the public declined markedly as it became evident that the Japanese might constitute as much of a labor and population threat as the Chinese had a decade earlier.

"Despite a growing atmosphere of hostility to further immigration, Japanese laborers, to the number of nearly 110,000 within a single decade, were brought into the Territory after annexation and women and children continued to arrive until the passage of the Exclusion Act in 1924." Reaching a peak in 1920, when they constituted 42 percent of the total, the proportion of Japanese in the total population declined in the thirties and by the sixties was about thirty percent.

During their years in Hawaiʻi, the Japanese rose from lowly plantation laborers who were severely discriminated against in the nineteenth century, to positions of prominence in the twentieth, especially as professionals in medicine, dentistry, education, law, and business. They suffered the most far-reaching cultural changes as immigrants' children were educated in American schools and became acculturated as American citizens. They suffered the greatest strains in World War II as Japan cruelly attacked Hawaiʻi at Pearl Harbor, and they emerged from that war, despite earlier suspicion and internment in concentration camps, as loyal and brave Americans. This was especially true of those young Nisei who served in the Armed Forces of the United States with distinction and with heroism.

After the war, another dramatic turn of events in the history of the Japanese-Americans of Hawaiʻi found them the leaders of a quiet revolution in which, through the constitutional means of the free election and the American system of government, they became the most powerful political element in Hawaiʻi and achieved what seemed to people in Hawaiʻi only a generation back as an utter impossibility. If it had even been considered in the past, the haole controlling element would have considered it a total disaster.

A remarkable haole was the instrument of this revolution in political power. His name was John Burns and his colleagues were George Ariyoshi, who followed Burns as Governor in 1974, thus becoming the first Governor of Japanese decent; Dan Inouye, elected United States Senator for Hawai'i in 1963; Spark Matsunaga, elected in 1963 as Representative to Congress and elected Senator in 1977; and Patsy Takemoto Mink, who first served in Congress from 1965 to 1977 and spent her life in politics. She was re-elected to Congress in 1990. Mrs. Mink was born to Japanese parents in one of the camps for sugar workers at Upper Paia.

Another child of Japanese immigrants, Toshio Ansai, played a key role in Maui politics for half a century. Born in 1908, Ansai grew up in Wailuku and worked hard even as a child.

Ansai was the fourth child of Kumataro and Kesayo Ansai, who emigrated from Fukushima province in Japan in the early 1900s to Papaiko on the Big Island. When the wet weather there exacerbated Kumataro's asthma condition, they moved to Maui, where he became a carpenter for the Wailuku Sugar Co.

The couple had left their daughter, Haruyo, with their parents in Japan. Now they sent for her, and had eight more children, three sons and five daughters. The family lived in Stable Camp, across from Molina's Bar in Wailuku. With an ailing father, all the children had to go to work at a young age and had little opportunity for education. The boys collected scraps for pigs and made tofu, eventually working for the plantation, and the girls sought work as domestics or with local businesses.

After eighth grade, Toshio got a job as a filing clerk at Wailuku Sugar Co. He continued to attend school whenever he could, impressing his bosses by his efforts to educate himself. Soon he was managing Waihee Farm and Dairy. In 1929 he married Ruth Shinayo Harimoto.

Ansai announced in 1934 that he would run for the County Board of Supervisors. A Republican, he was one of the first Nisei to run for public office. Well known as a leader in recreation and sports, with a wife willing to campaign as hard as he did, Ansai was elected and continued to be re-elected until 1942, when he declined to run because he was busy with defense work.

When Americans of Japanese ancestry were allowed to enlist in early 1943, Ansai was among the first volunteers. At age 35, he was one of the oldest of the new soldiers, and took a leadership role in the 442nd Regimental Combat Team.

Back home on furlough in 1945, Ansai described the prejudice the Nisei soldiers faced as newly arrived troops in Mississippi. Nevertheless, toughened by years of outdoor work and sports, the soldiers passed an Army fitness test with near-perfect scores and went on to distinguish themselves in fierce battles in Europe.

"It is going to be hard for these boys to take off their uniforms, put on civies and settle down," First Sgt. Ansai told the Rotary Club of Maui. "The war has changed everybody including the people here on Maui; you may not realize it but the war and changed conditions have affected all of you; the boys are no different."

After the war, Ansai became the industrial relations manager for Wailuku Sugar. He was elected to the Territorial Senate in 1948, though he spent most of the campaign in the hospital being treated for problems from his war wounds. For most of the next 30 years, he was either in the Senate or in county government. He lobbied actively for statehood and helped get state funds to put in roads and water lines when Kahului was subdivided to create "Dream City."

He finished his long political career after his retirement from Wailuku Sugar in 1972 by serving four terms on the County Council and then being appointed to the Maui County Planning Commission. Toshio Ansai died in 1993.

THE FILIPINOS

In 1907, Japan was closed as a source of laborers and several of the smaller ethnic groups were introduced to Hawai'i after that, partly as foils to the large Japanese population. Nearly 6,000 Puerto Ricans had arrived in 1901, about 8,000 Koreans in 1904 and

1905, while an equal number of Spaniards had been recruited by 1913, though several thousand of these latter emigrated to California. Puerto Ricans remained and reproduced and still constitute an important, though small, segment of the Hawaiian population, having intermarried extensively.

The Filipinos were the last of the ethnic groups to enter the Territory, nearly 120,000 being imported as plantation laborers during the period 1907-1931. The strike of the Japanese workers in 1909 had given the planters a bad scare and also good reason to seek relief from the near monopoly of plantation labor by the Japanese.

It was no longer thought necessary to use immigration to solve the population problem, and Filipinos were recruited mainly for economic reasons, as is suggested by the extreme disproportion of males to females–which exceeded four to one in the first contingents and later reached a ratio of 19 to 1 during the years 1924 to 1930.

Although for much of the century the new immigrants from the Philippines filled the jobs that more established residents were no longer willing to handle, many advanced to positions of importance in business and the professions.

A. B. Sevilla

In 1928 the S.S. *President Taft* arrived in Honolulu. On board was a nineteen-year-old Filipino whose voice would, one day, be an alarm clock to thousands of Mauians. His name was A. B. Sevilla. Young Sevilla spent one night on Oʻahu, then took an inter-island steamer to Kahului. "I remember thinking it was a lot cooler here than back home. I was surprised about the island. The trees were all small, not really tall like home." Sevilla was not on a contract and paid his own way to Hawaiʻi. His family had borrowed money on their rice paddies to pay his passage. Once here, however, he signed a three-year contract that paid one dollar a day for twenty-five working days a month and fare back to the Philippines at the end of the contract. It took him until 1966 to collect on the last portion of his contract, but the Hawaiian Sugar Planters Association stood behind their agreement and paid his airfare to the Philippines.

Sevilla's career on the plantation was spotty. He tried the railroad but quit "because there was no future in it. I wanted to work in the canefields." He tried to get a job in the mill but was turned down there. "So many days I had no job—nobody wanted me. The camp police found out I wasn't working and came around and wanted to know why. In those days the police checked if you said you were sick or weren't on the job."

For a time Sevilla worked in the engine room at the Pu'unene mill, then applied for a job in a store owned by Alexander and Baldwin. "The mill boss said I couldn't work for the store without approval, so that job was out for the time being. I didn't go to work anymore (at the mill) and finally the mill boss gave up and I got the job at the store and worked in the wholesale section for seven and a half years."

Sevilla tried to get further education, played in an orchestra, wrote a book in Ilocano about the Filipino immigrants, and in 1938 opened his own store in Wailuku.

"Life was hard [before he opened the store]. Because I'm a Filipino they thought I should have less money. You can't do that, I thought." He went to night school in the thirties and learned bookkeeping and typing, and in 1947, when Maui got its first radio station, Sevilla joined the staff. He became Maui's first home-grown broadcasting personality, a position he held until he retired in 1976. A. B. Sevilla died in 1995.

These stories of individuals who came to Maui from other countries and worked their way through difficult times, hard work and sacrifice, gave their children education and a better life, could be multiplied by thousands. These people accepted their lot and persevered in what, for them, was a strange and alien land; they adapted, survived discrimination, poverty, power struggles, massive social upheavals, and the rapid technological changes, to contribute the work of their hands, the sweat of their brows, and eventually the creativity of their minds to this island home of many peoples.

GROWING UP HAWAIIAN

The story of a man who grew up Hawaiian on Maui may give insight into another island lifestyle as it was adapted to the social changes of the twentieth century. This man is Charles Pili Keau, a citizen of Maui who represents in his attitudes, works, and community services, many of the best aspects of the survival (and revival) of traditional values.

His cooperation and interest in Hawaiian history and prehistory (mainly archaeology) have added significant scope to the story of his life, especially as Charlie expresses a feeling of social obligation to his fellow citizens. He has said that his aim is to work "toward preserving the Hawaiian people's heritage and a serene island existence for everyone."

Charlie is probably about as pure Hawaiian as can be found on the islands. One greatgrandfather was Portuguese from the Azores and it was this single ancestor from whom the family took its devout Catholic faith. His paternal grandparents were pure Hawaiian, named Pili and Koleka Kenui. His father was Charles Pili, and the family lived by the sea near the heiaus at Paukukalo. Father Pili was a cowboy and later a carpenter for the county. Mr. Pili knew the "ocean scent," the currents, the richest fishing grounds, the types of fish, and the methods of catching these essential Hawaiian foods. Although he died when Charlie was only two, this knowledge was passed on by his uncle Antone, the brother of Mrs. Annie Faustino Pili, Charlie's mother.

After her husband's death, Mrs. Pili married David Keau, member of a large and respected Hawaiian family. They had three children and adopted a Korean child named Edwin Pung. Charlie took the name of his stepfather.

Charlie's mother served as the great bond of the family. She was the organizer and loving disciplinarian. She told the children about the traditional Hawaiian customs, the old legends, the ancestors. She was very active in the Hawaiian membership of St. Anthony's Church. For the feast days of Corpus Christi, Mrs. Keau made Hawaiian foods. She was well-loved in the community and known, too, for her teaching of quilt-making to the parish women.

Among his peers, Charlie gained a better understanding of the cultures of many ethnic groups on Maui. His best friend, Soichi Takayama, would bring a lunch of sushi and vegetables especially for Charlie. Charlie would trade some poi, fish, or breadfruit with his pal. He learned the eating habits, dress customs, and social ways of his Filipino, Portuguese, Puerto Rican, Japanese, and Chinese friends. In his elementary classes there seemed to be an even distribution in the numbers of different ethnic students.

Charles believed while he was a young boy and during the 1930s, that "life was truly beautiful, really great times." He felt the islands' people were very happy in their simple lifestyles. They worked hard, and they had few luxuries or worries. Although the ethnic groups were segregated within the camp housing tracts, there existed a big family whose reality embraced the Aloha spirit. If one group sponsored a party everyone was invited. If a wedding ceremony was planned, then everyone contributed their *kokua* or help, and everyone enjoyed the fruits of lengthy preparation.

"People brought their fish catch, harvested fruits and vegetables, and handmade crafts to the Saturday flea market on Market Street in Wailuku. A person knew almost every other person in town. Whether the people went to the beach or shopping all day, they usually never locked their house doors. Any friend was welcome to enter and to eat food even when no one was at home. Aloha meant what is mine is yours; a selfless favor really came from the heart and not the mouth. People were not suspicious of others. Nearly every person was inwardly content and friendly."

With the start of World War II in 1941, Charlie had to quit school to help support his family. Charles was drafted in 1945, at age eighteen, and cleared the course of basic training at Camp Hood, Texas. As an Infantryman in the Army, he continued with special training for the Army Transportation Corps at Camp Plauche in New Orleans.

Charles Keau feels that the war truly revolutionized Hawai'i in several ways. The war had exposed Hawai'i to the rest of the world through those who travelled abroad and by serving as the major base of the United States in the Pacific. The people had won a high degree of self-confidence and felt capable of governing themselves. The people no longer wanted the nonrepresentative, paternalistic system which had dominated the islands for over one hundred years.

Charlie feels that during this time many islanders moved farther away from their parents' lifestyles. Old customs and a great family and community love were dissolving as people sought more individualism and stylism. People locked their doors and the Aloha spirit decayed, while some persons prejudged each other more often by appearance or possessions. A sense of tolerance, the willingness to accept others who do not hold a particular tradition or who look differently, still exists uniquely in Hawai'i. Yet Charlie feels that modern economic thinking had changed the old quality of Aloha.

In 1948, Charles was at home on Maui when he went to work for Maui Pineapple Company. In 1955, he went to Eniewetok in the Marshall Islands to work on the atomic energy project on the construction labor force. Returning to Maui in 1956, he married a girl of Spanish descent and together they raised six fine children.

In 1971, Charlie began to work in the State Parks and Recreation program to restore historical sites on state land on Maui. The first site that was cleared and marked for visiting was at the two half-destroyed heiaus in upper Paukukalo, where Charlie had played as a boy with his brothers picking mangoes and swimming in the stream below the stone walls. Charlie felt privileged to work with the anthropologists and archaeologists of the Bishop Museum, especially Dr. Kenneth Emory, Dr. Rob Hommon, and Dr. Yoshiko Sinoto, with whom he worked on the archaeological sites at La Pérouse Bay. He also worked with Leslie Bruce of Maui, and especially learned to love archaeology while working with two young researchers who taught him how to map and draw archaeological layouts, and how to work carefully in the field. Together they exchanged new and old knowledge about the Polynesian heritage, and Charlie was able to enhance their findings with many peculiarities that he knew were found in the heiaus, the village ruins, or the artifacts.

Charlie is an active member of the Maui Historical Society, took part in the Society's inventory of pre-historical sites on Maui, assisted in the Bishop Museum's survey of ancient sites for the developments at Wailea and Kapalua. In 1974 he became a maintenance man for the County with primary assignment at Kepaniwai Park in the 'Iao Valley. He retired from the County Parks Department in 1992.

In an interview in 1977, Charlie had this to say about the native Hawaiians:

"I feel that the people are gaining confidence and want to articulate their concern about a rapidly growing population on the homeland. There was a gap between 1920 and 1970 when Hawaiians wouldn't speak up because they feared that people would misinterpret them. People would doubt what the wise folks knew. For instance, a local man believes a special place is kapu, or sacred, and he tries to tell someone. The listener may think–this man is silly, superstitious, or trying to scare me. What the local man really means to convey are attitudes of respect, carefulness, and preservation. He means to say, 'put all things back where you found them and keep a modest vibration within your heart.'"

Charlie's perspective seems to embrace the uniqueness of Hawaiian history, tradition, and today's modern life and society. Charlie is committed to the aloha within everyone and to the power of the *'aina*, the land.

THE HAOLES

Part of the story of the haole ruling chiefs of Maui in the nineteenth century and earlier twentieth century has been told in the chapter on sugar, though it must be pointed out parenthetically that the word "sugar" alone does not describe the power structure, it only symbolized it. It was sugar–its planting and production–that was the basis for the whole power structure which developed, and in which those who owned and controlled the sugar industry gradually came to control first its refining, then its marketing, then the shipping which carried it to market, then the supply of all its accessory supplies, its insurance, and then the banks which supplied the capital, and the ownership of the vast acreages of the best lands on every island of the chain. With this enormous economic power, a veritable ruling kingdom of sugar arose which then added political power to the oligarchy.

A so-called Big Five emerged. It was composed of A & B, American Factors, Castle & Cooke, C. Brewer & Company, and Theo Davies and Company. Dillingham made it a "Big Sixth."

This group controlled 75 percent of the sugar crop by 1910, and 96 percent by 1933. The same handful of men who controlled the Big Five ran the government of Hawai'i.

Every one of the Big Five had at least one direct descendant of a missionary on its board, and Alexander & Baldwin had six– William Alexander, Harry A. Baldwin, F. F. Baldwin, William O. Smith, A. C. Alexander, A. C. Castle and J. P. Cooke. "Those names and others from the missionary family… appeared on the boards of almost every important firm that did business at Honolulu…. Even the 'Big Sixth,' Walter F. Dillingham…was related to the missionary family through his mother."

"A member of the United States Attorney General's staff drew a diagram of interlocking directorates in 1932, and the result was a picture of lines of power and influence such as Walter Murray Gibson, Claus Spreckels and King Ka-lakaua would never have dreamed of in their most extravagant moments."

Between 1900 and 1940 eight out of every ten men elected to the Territorial legislature were Republicans. Very large sums were spent by the Big Five to elect Republicans, and the legislators could hardly help being considerate of their benefactors. The Big Five members did not mind being accused of paternalism. After all, the wages of plantation workers in Hawai'i were higher than anywhere else in the world, and laborers' living conditions improved after the strikes of 1909 and 1920. Management was ready by then to concede that a happy worker was less likely to strike than a disgruntled one.

The positions of power and prestige enjoyed by most haoles, almost from the first arrival of Captain Cook, have meant a very different experience in Hawai'i as compared to any other immigrant group. The proportion of the population who could occupy such positions of influence and prestige was necessarily limited, and no large numbers of haoles were reported in the censuses throughout the nineteenth century.

It was not until Hawai'i began to figure prominently as a military and tourist frontier that their numbers and their proportion of the total population rose markedly.

THE MASTER OF ROSE RANCH

Although it is not typical of the lifestyle of all the wealthy planters in the nineteenth century, a story that is told of James Makee of Rose Ranch on Maui illustrates something of their philosophy and shows a sharp contrast to the lifestyles of the immigrant peoples who worked for them.

Makee prided himself more on knowing how to live than on knowing how to make money. Over the years, he put about a million dollars into his plantation at Ulupalakua on the slopes of Haleakala, and the thousand acres he kept under crop yielded him 800 tons of sugar in a good year. At the same time, he cultivated the good life on a grand scale. His rambling plantation house was ringed with guest cottages, and he liked to keep the cottages filled and the guests content. He bought a piano for his parlor, an organ for his chapel, and outside he built a billiard room, a tennis court, and a bowling alley with one small kanaka boy to tend each pin. His gardens were lavish, and his guests were invited to canter on horseback among thousands of trees imported to give variety to the landscape, along with birds to sing in them. Makee knew how to put on a show for royalty, but handled most occasions with an understated grace.

Once, while the common seamen of a touring warship were enjoying barbequed beef at Makee's private landing, Makee himself was serving fowl to the officers in the dining hall of the plantation house. After the main course, the admiral, full of good food and good cheer, remarked that his host was fit to carve a peacock at a

Roman feast, and Makee replied nonchalantly, "Gentlemen, the birds you have just eaten—were peacocks!"

The days of control by a small group were long gone by the end of the twentieth century. Maui's political and economic system had long been open to all races.

Even in the days when the Caucasian plantation owners and the Republican Party controlled much of life on Maui, Hawaiians were a force in local politics. Samuel Kalama, for example, took office as chairman of the County Board of Supervisors in 1913 and left his mark on Maui through extensive public works during his twenty years in office.

Toshio Ansai, an early example of a Nisei politician, was a rarity in the second half of the century—a Republican official of Japanese ancestry in a time when the Democratic Party was the increasingly powerful political home of most Hawai'i residents of Japanese ethnicity.

Two influential mayors of the last decades of the twentieth century, Elmer Cravalho and Hannibal Tavares, were of Portuguese descent. They were followed by Linda Lingle, a Caucasian woman of Jewish heritage, who held the office during the 1990s as Maui's first female chief executive.

Lingle was one of many new Mauians who had been born elsewhere. The increase in the haole population began in the 1950s, accelerated after statehood in 1959, and continued through the end of the century.

Other ethnic groups also joined the mix, including Tongans, Samoans, and Southeast Asians. Spanish-speaking immigrants began to arrive in large numbers in 1990, with their numbers growing to an estimated 10,000 by the year 2000. Though many of the Hispanic newcomers found jobs in the tourist industry, particularly on the west side, their initial influx followed a familiar pattern. Like many ethnic groups before them, the Spanish-speakers first came as a group when pineapple plantations imported them in response to a labor shortage.

CHAPTER 10

MAUI REMEMBERED: 1900-1950

The calm surface of life on the Island of Maui in the decades before 1940 was hardly rippled. Early in the century several famous authors visited briefly and wrote articles that were read nationwide.

Mark Twain had been enchanted with the Islands in 1866 when he wrote his often-quoted phrase, "the loveliest fleet of islands that lies anchored in any ocean." Half a century later, Jack London, then America's most famous author, fell under Hawai'i's spell and wrote two volumes of short stories based on the Islands.

Jack London visited Maui, where he was the guest of Louis von Tempsky, manager of the Haleakala Ranch. Louis' young daughter, Armine, an aspiring writer, showed London some of her manuscripts. He told her that it was ìmostly tripeî but that she had talent. He encouraged her to continue. Armine von Tempsky became a successful writer, especially with her best-selling autobiography, *Born in Paradise*.

Millions of readers were enchanted by the romantic life on a Maui ranch, but not one reader in ten thousand had any clear idea where Maui was or even that such a place existed in fact.

The first World War hardly touched the quiet life of the island. People remembered that supplies of flour and other commodities were scarce and that they rather enjoyed having to fall back on the island's own resources. Schoolchildren were taught to care for "home gardens," flour was made out of dried bananas and people "made do" with foods and materials which the old Hawaiians had always used effectively. Maui lost one man in World War I.

Some German sailors stranded in Hawai'i were removed from American ships. These men were imprisoned; some were paroled and placed on Kipahulu Plantation, Maui, where they remained at work until the restrictions were removed in the summer of 1919.

After World War I, a select few very well-heeled visitors came to vacation or spend the winter in one of the two or three existing hotels at Waikiki. Some of them flew in small amphibians to see the volcanoes on Hawai'i, but Maui was seldom, if ever, on their itinerary. In 1936, Pam Am inaugurated the "China Clippers" for regular weekly flights from San Francisco to Honolulu. These flying boats, cruising at the high altitude of 10,000 feet, took eighteen hours each way. The people of the islands were still traveling by small inter-island steamers, a rough trip but vastly improved over the uncomfortable and even dangerous voyages between islands in the late nineteenth and early twentieth centuries.

WORLD WAR II

The Japanese attack on Pearl Harbor was a terrific shock to the people of Maui. They were stunned, then galvanized into action. Still it was some time before beaches could be barricaded and gun emplacements prepared at potential landing places. A Japanese invasion was fully expected.

A submarine lobbed a few shells into Kahului Harbor, a couple of them making holes in two or three places. None of them exploded. On January 25, 1942, another submarine torpedoed and sank the transport *Gen. Royal T. Frank* in the channel between Maui and Hawai'i. Twenty-nine persons were lost while thirty-three survivors made it to land.

A terrible accident the following year took the lives of a score of servicemen who were training on Maui. Two Navy bombers on a training flight collided in the air over Maui on December 7, 1943. Both pilots parachuted to safety but their respective radiomen were killed. A bomb carried by one of the planes, loosened by the impact, fell and exploded in the midst of a group of Marines, killing twenty and injuring twenty-nine. The news of this disaster was only briefly mentioned on the inside pages of the *Honolulu Star-Bulletin*. No details were given. The accident occurred on the second anniversary of Pearl Harbor.

The Japanese invasion of Maui never materialized but the island became an important training, staging, and rest area for the Marines in the Pacific.

THE FOURTH MARINE DIVISION

Robert Sherrod, author and war correspondent attached to the Fourth Marine Division wrote in 1946:

> There is no doubt in my mind that the historians will decide, when the final returns are in, that the Central Pacific was the main stroke against Japan. This was the campaign where the Fourth fought all its battles—at Roi-Namur, Saipan-Tinian, and Iwo Jima—and fought them as magnificently as Americans ever fought. . . It was in combat but a total of 63 days…yet …no division participated in more violent combat than did the Fourth …the Fourth set something of a record in making four beachheads–all of them bitterly opposed–in less than 13 months.

Yet, in many ways the Fourth was more fortunate than some of its sister divisions. Its zone of action was exclusively in the Central Pacific; jungles, oppressive heat, and tropical disease were not part of its experience; casualties from malaria, filariasis, and jungle rot were practically unknown; it was based, between operations, in "the next best place to the States–the Island of Maui." They were not so fortunate where enemy bullets and shells were concerned. Sixty-three days of merciless but futile enemy opposition accounted for probably the highest casualty rate of any Marine division. During the four operations in which the division was engaged, a total of 81,718 men saw action one or more times. Robert Sherrod wrote, "…the price the Division had to pay was heavy–as it must be on small, vital targets. It amounted to about 75 percent of the original divisional strength (17,086). It takes men to stand such losses and come up as determined as ever. The Fourth had the men."

Even before the Fourth Marine Division landed on Maui where a base camp was being prepared for them, they got their first glimpse of the island on the way to the Marshalls. Their transports put in to Lahaina Roads for a day of provisioning. It was January 1944 and the ships had left San Diego for a secret destination, the first attack in the Pacific to be mounted directly from the mainland United States. They had trained at Camp Pendleton, California, and knew only that they were on their way to first combat under the name "Operation Flintlock." As they looked longingly at the green fields, the palm trees and the mountains and beaches of the island, they did not know that they would be landing here a little more than a month later after the battle of Roi-Namur. For those who survived, Maui would be "home base" for the next two years.

When they returned to Maui from Roi-Namur in late February 1944, the Division had lost one hundred and ninety men, and five hundred forty-seven were wounded during the brief twenty-four-hour engagement. Two hundred and sixty-four Japanese prisoners had been captured and 3,472 enemy troops lay buried on tiny Roi-Namur. Overnight, the "green" Fourth had become veterans.

CAMP MAUI

The transports landed the Marines, 16,000 of them, at Kahului Harbor whence they were carried in a long convoy of trucks from the docks through Paia and Makawao to their camp at Kokomo. Three times in fifteen months the Fourth Division made this journey from the Kahului docks twelve miles up the hill to camp, and each time Maui seemed more beautiful to them.

Camp Maui gradually took shape as base for both combat training and rest and recreation.

"Slowly, in spite of the mud and the wind and the rain and the first pangs of homesickness for the States—slowly, civilization began to grow out of barren fields. Buildings went up for offices, tents for living quarters; mess halls were constructed and roads carved through the mire. Post Exchanges opened up with supplies of 'pogey bait',* tobacco, and enough beer for two bottles per man a night. Movie screens and stages were built in each regimental area. Ball diamonds were laid out and boxing rings constructed. Company libraries were opened, and Marines had their choice of 73 magazines. Chaplains, somehow, procured enough lumber for chapels; electric lights were installed in all tents; public-address systems were wired into the company areas and used for piping announcements and the latest music to Marines. Within a few months Camp Maui had become a relatively decent place to live." There were nightly movies, in the rain before a theater was erected. Hula girls tried to introduce the Marines to some of the old Hawaiian culture, and the Fourth organized its own show which became famous in the Pacific first as "The Fubar Follies," later as the "Just 4 Fun Show" when it toured the "foxhole circuit."

On April 1, 1944, General Harry Schmidt made the first of several mass presentations of the Purple Heart during the Division's stay on Maui. Thousands of Marines were to receive this medal at one time or another at Camp Maui.

On April 26, 1944, Admiral Nimitz journeyed to Camp Maui to present awards to men who had earned them at Roi-Namur. Twice again on Maui, mass awards for bravery were presented to men of the Fourth–after Saipan-Tinian, and after Iwo Jima. Each time there were fewer of the original men of the Fourth to hear the words of commendation. On July 4, 1945, a parade was held on the Camp Maui airstrip, at which 714 men of the Division were decorated.

As the war rolled on, Maui more and more became "home" to the men of the Fourth. USOs in Haiku, Makawao, Kahului, and Wailuku furnished hot showers, games, swimming, tennis, dances, and refreshments. It was here that Marines met the girls of Maui, friendships were formed and romances blossomed.

The terrain and beaches of the island provided excellent training ground for the battles ahead. Replacements arrived, and the Army's Jungle Training Center was opened to Marines. Exercises and training hikes utilized some of Maui's more rugged terrain. The thirteen-mile hike through the crater was a trial for the sturdiest leg muscles. All the Division's amphibious maneuvers for the Marianas

---

* "Pogey bait" in Navy parlance is candy.

and Iwo Jima operations were held off Ma'alaea Bay and along the beaches and kiawe jungles east of the bay.

In May 1944, during rehearsals for the assault on Saipan, held at Ma'alaea Bay and Kaho'olawe, an LCT in which Marines were sleeping was pitched overboard from the deck of LST-485 by heavy seas, owing to insufficient lashings, and nineteen men were lost.

A total of forty-seven training areas, many belonging to the Army, were shared by the units in training. Army facilities on Maui consisted of a jungle training center, a village fighting course, a cave fighting course, and an infiltration course. The fortified jungle position consisted of twenty-two pillboxes and emplacements well concealed in bamboo groves, under the roots of banyan trees, and in thick undergrowth.

There were numerous other training areas. The author of the *The Fourth Marine Division During World War II,* wrote, "Families in the Island threw open their doors to the Marines...citizens of Maui proved that 'Aloha' was more than a word. The Fourth soon became 'Maui's Own.'...Who will ever forget the reception that Maui gave the Fourth when it returned from Iwo? It is not an exaggeration to say that no division anywhere received a more heart-warming welcome when it came back from battle."

Every returning Marine on that occasion received a little pamphlet. Reading that message from the people of Maui, the returning Marines must have felt how good it was to be alive and to be back in their temporary island home. They had been through their worst battle of all–Iwo Jima. As the transports drew up to their moorings at Kahului Harbor, the men stood quietly along the rails; the bands lined up in front of a welcoming crowd; the hula girls stood waiting to begin the dance. One who was there remembered a hush, a moment of stunned silence...then the band played *Aloha Oe* and the cheering could be heard twelve miles up the mountain where Camp Maui was ready to receive them for the last time. Some on Maui thirty years later recalled the message which read:

"ALOHA. Hi, you Marines! Welcome home! It's no 'snow job' when we tell you that the servicemen and women and the civilians of Maui are throwing this big shindig for you because we think you're just about the greatest guys that ever landed on this Island. When the news came over the radio that the Marines had hit Iwo Jima, everybody asked the same question, 'Are the Maui Marines there?' Then we heard the news flash that you and a lot of other Marines were in their pitching. After that, nothing else that happened seemed to matter very much. We don't need to tell you that everyone from Hana to Lahaina is mighty proud of you. And when we read that you had named that first street 'Maui Boulevard,' we were practically bursting at the seams.

"So welcome to Maui–the old friends and the new! Welcome to 'Iao Valley and Haleakala–to the rainbows and the rain (that everlasting rain at Camp Maui)–the steaks and the banana splits–the pineapples and the poi–the carnation leis and the steel guitars. But, most important of all, welcome back to all the folks on Maui who think it might be a pretty good idea to add a new word to the famous slogan, MAUI NO KA OI ('Maui is the best') and let the world know it is now, MAUI MARINES NO KA OI!" It was signed, "The People of Maui."

At Iwo, 1,462 of their comrades were killed, 344 more had died of wounds and 7,292 of them had been wounded. Total casualties for the Fourth Division of Marines alone in their sixty-three days of combat, amounted to 2,774 killed in action, 524 died of wounds and 14,424 wounded. Strength of the Division averaged between seventeen and eighteen thousand during 1943, 1944, and 1945, so that the total casualties (including wounded) amounted to more than 75 percent of the assigned divisional strength!

From April 1945, when they arrived back from Iwo, until the Fourth Marines left for San Diego and deactivation in October-November 1945, the finishing touches were put on Camp Maui. Roads were paved, frame buildings took the place of tents, and a number of auditoriums were built, "finally making it possible to see movies without getting wet." New athletic fields were laid out, one of them named for the Division's football ace, Howard "Smiley" Johnson, who had been killed at Iwo. The Fourth Marine Division's historian wrote, "For the old timers who had slogged around in the mud when the Division first came to Maui, it didn't seem quite right. They weren't kidding anybody though. Everyone enjoyed it, for Maui had become just about the next best place to home."

Soon after the Japanese surrender, the Fourth was selected as the first Marine division to return to the States. The elation that followed was mixed with a pang of sadness. The men of the Fourth had become genuinely fond of Maui and its people. And the people of Maui gave them a succession of farewells between October 6 when the first contingent boarded the Cartier Escort *Attu* at Kahului and November 3 when the Carrier Escort *Kassan Bay* sailed with the last of the Division.

On reaching San Diego, the various units were sent to Camp Pendleton for demobilization. The date was November 28, 1945. Two years, three months, and thirteen days after its activation, the Fourth Marine Division was no more.

Camp Maui was also "deactivated" and typically there was the same waste of material that took place in so many armed forces installations at the end of World War II. In a few cases, half-tracks along with heaps of other gear were pushed over the side of the gulch or burned. Even the worthy little vehicle, the Jeep, was disposed of, only a few failing into civilian hands, and thirty-five years later still occasionally seen running about the boondocks of the island.

In 1980, some of "Maui's Own" returned for the dedication of a park on the site of their camp.

The Men From Maui

Maui's own sons were serving in World War II, some giving their lives courageously especially in the European theater where the 100th Infantry Battalion and the 442nd Regimental Combat Team became heroes of the Italian and French campaigns. In Italy the famous 442nd was at the front four weeks without a break, getting only two hours' sleep a night and spending the rest of each day defeating battle-hardened elite German troops. Then the 442nd was sent to France, where in thirty-five minutes it smashed a Nazi stronghold that had defied other Allied forces for five weeks. By the end of the war, the unit had been engaged in seven major campaigns and won seven Presidential citations at the cost of 9,486 casualties.

Individual members of the 442nd won a total of 18,143 decorations including the Congressional Medal of Honor and fifty-two Distinguished Service Crosses. No other unit of the armed forces established a comparable war record.

These fighting units were manned by young Americans of Japanese ancestry (A.J.A.'s), the *Nisei*, or second generation Americans. One hundred and twenty-six men from Maui, whose permanent population was then about 47,000, gave their lives in World War II, not all of them A.J.A.'s. The roster at Maui's War Memorial Gymnasium lists the names Rosario and Alborado, several Wongs, a Prescott, a Polansky, and a Hoopii, among a majority of Japanese names. The monument there reads:

In Memoriam
*In honor of all Americans of the County of Maui
who died in the service of their country
that beauty and freedom of our country be preserved
for all humanity*

THE POST-WAR PERIOD

After the war, the Japanese in Hawai'i were fully recognized not only as loyal, but as patriotic Americans. The young men of the *Nisei* who fought so bravely abroad returned to Hawai'i to be received by cheering crowds and grateful families. Many of them took advantage of the G.I. Bill to further their education, becoming prominent businessmen, teachers, lawyers, doctors, dentists, government officials, and political leaders. It was with their help and leadership that a new political power was forged out of the Democratic Party.

The unions, already powerful in Hawai'i, began to organize more effectively for political action as the professional core of a new political machine took power in the Territory from the long-established Republican Party and its stronghold among the Big Five.

On Maui, the local governing body was the Board of Supervisors headed by a County Chairman and Executive Officer who was, in effect, the chief officer of the unique four-island county of Maui. For many years, the Board had been dominated by the Republican hierarchy. For a time before and after World War II, the man who wielded the political power was the Territorial Senator, Harold W. Rice, a son-in-law of H. P. Baldwin.

Years later, Eddie Tam, Rice's secretary, told the following story to Bob Krauss of the *Honolulu Advertiser*: After about fifteen years Eddie was earning a salary of $35.00 a week. When he asked for a raise, the Senator said, "I tell you what I'll do Eddie. I'll run you for the Board of Supervisors. It's only a part time job but it'll give you a little extra income."

In 1942, Eddie Tam was elected to the Board as a Republican. In 1944, Senator Rice switched parties and ran as a Democrat. Eddie switched, too, and won again. By this time he began to realize that he had political power in his own right. He never lost an election after that.

In 1948, Eddie and the Senator had a falling out, Eddie quit or was fired as the Senator's secretary, and thereupon decided to run for the Maui County Chairmanship without Senator Rice's blessing. He won easily and Maui County had a new political power.

For eighteen years Eddie Tam opened the Maui County Fair, gave out Boy Scout awards (and an average of two keys to Maui every week), led the Whaling Spree Parade, greeted important visitors at the airport, feuded with political opponents, and sang the praises of Maui to anyone who would listen.

He stood only five feet five inches in his two-tone golfing shoes. His head barely cleared the steering wheel of his Cadillac, the back window of which carried a sign "Mayor Eddie Tam says Thank You."

The sign was put there following the 1958 election in which Tam won his sixth term as County Chairman by nearly 3,000 votes. He was immensely popular on Maui and two other signs are a clue to his success. A sign outside his office door read: "Courteous service to the public is the guiding principle of this office." Another hanging in the Board of Supervisors' meeting room read: "You can't sell peanuts at the end of a parade."

Eddie Tam was born of immigrant parents from China and never got beyond the ninth grade in school. He laid the foundations for his political career by managing orchestras which provided entertainment for community projects from highway dedications to campaign rallies.

He was a one-man visitors' bureau, especially when traveling to the mainland. Each trip, he took along hundreds of greeting cards and invited everyone he met to come to Maui. In 1954 during a Lions convention in Madison Square Garden in New York City, he gave away gallons of pineapple juice, 34,000 cubes of Hawaiian sugar and 40,000 vanda orchids.

Eddie Tam was still holding the office of County Chairman in December 1966 when he suddenly died of a heart attack. The headline in the *Honolulu Advertiser* was, "Maui Won't Be The Same Without 'Friendly Eddie.' "

A special election was called to elect Eddie Tam's successor.

A NEW KIND OF HIGH CHIEF

A young man from the tiny village of Paia, through brains, hard work, and administrative and political skills had risen to leadership in the Legislature of the Territory of Hawai'i. His name was Elmer Cravalho and, at the time of Eddie Tam's death, he was Speaker of the House of Representatives in Honolulu. He decided to return to Maui to stand election for the County Chairman's job. He won by the narrow margin of 139 votes.

Cravalho's grandparents were Portuguese immigrants from the island of San Miguel in the Azores and his grandfather came as a laborer for the sugar plantation. His father was born in one of the camps which the plantation maintained for its workers. The elder Cravalho was a teacher for forty-three years in the Maui schools.

Elmer Franklin Cravalho was born in 1926, the fifth of eight children. He grew up wanting to be an educator and, for eight years before he began his political career, he taught elementary classes on Maui.

His concern with social growth drew him into politics. In 1954 Cravalho became Chairman of the Democratic Party on Maui. He won his seat in the House in the same year and led the ticket. That became a habit as he was re-elected to the House every time, continuing each time to lead the ticket. He was a favorite of the late Governor Burns who helped Cravalho get things done for Maui. In 1956 Governor Burns asked him to run for Lieutenant Governor, but he declined.

Cravalho's first election forced him out of the classroom. A Territorial law prohibited elected officials from holding other public jobs.

He found odd jobs for a time but soon began to move into several business ventures, especially the business of ranching. Careful investments and clever management succeeded and by 1965, Cravalho's company, Maui Factors, was running as many as a thousand head of cattle. At the same time he acquired land Upcountry where many of his fellow Portuguese lived and operated their ranches and where Cravalho had close family connections. He bought or leased more land and his interest and experience in ranching and agriculture deepened. His business interests had made him financially independent by the time he took office as Mayor of Maui County.

Cravalho's twelve years in the mayor's office were times of major development, guided by the mayor's firm hand. While he saw the importance of tourism, he also insisted that agriculture must be protected. He sought to keep tourism development confined to specific areas of the island, with the focus on the well-heeled visitor. This approach brought prosperity to the county and its government.

In 1979, a few months after beginning a new term, Cravalho announced that he would resign. Though he insisted then and later that his motives for leaving office were entirely personal, there were charges in the ensuing special election that he had left because of difficulties with federally funded sewer projects. Cravalho came out of political retirement in 1990 to run unsuccessfully for mayor against Republican Linda Lingle. Cravalho went on to serve as chairman of the Maui County Board of Water Supply.

Elmer Cravalho was succeeded in office by Hannibal Tavares, another strong mayor of Portuguese descent. Born in Makawao in

1919, Tavares entered politics in 1954, serving several terms on the Board of Supervisors. He worked as a teacher, a policeman and a public relations man in the sugar industry.

When Cravalho suddenly resigned as mayor in 1979, Tavares won in a resounding victory against seventeen other candidates despite his being out of politics for twenty years. He was elected two more times, in 1982 and 1986. A big man with a booming voice, he was a familiar sight at community events.

Tavares said that he considered his "monument" to be Maui's county master plan, the first such document in Hawai'i and one of the first in the nation, which he spearheaded during his time on the Board of Supervisors. When he became mayor, he said it was a job he had trained for all his life, and clearly one he relished.

After he left office, Tavares was named chairman of the Kahoolawe Island Conveyance Commission, which facilitated the return of the battered island to the state. Tavares died in 1998 at age 78.

Linda Lingle, Tavares' successor, was the youngest person ever elected mayor in Maui County's history, the county's first woman mayor, and the first non-Maui-born person to hold the office.

Lingle was Maui's mayor for most of the 1990s, a trying time of tight budgets. Her businesslike attitude was often credited for helping Maui get through the recessionary years of the nineties in better shape than Hawai'i's other counties.

Born in 1953 in St. Louis, Missouri, Lingle graduated with a degree in journalism and moved to Hawai'i in 1975. In 1976, she moved to Moloka'i and started the *Moloka'i Free Press.* Through her newspaper work she developed an interest in the issues, and ran successfully for the Moloka'i Council seat in 1980 and in the next two elections. In 1985 she moved to Kihei and won an at-large council seat. In 1990, she became the first person ever to beat Elmer Cravalho in an electoral race.

Following her two terms in the mayor's office, Lingle ran against incumbent Gov. Ben Cayetano, with far more success in many would have expected. She did lose, however, and moved to O'ahu, where she remained a force in Republican politics as chairperson of the Hawai'i Republican Party.

CHAPTER II

MAUI AFTER STATEHOOD: 1959–1979

The boom that began in the sixties brought about remarkable changes on an island that, at statehood in 1959, was still a relatively unknown speck in the Pacific Ocean, a community of 36,000 people.

Mainland influences already had begun to have an impact. World War II brought the outside world to Maui. Islanders who had lived through the changes of those days, whether at home or as soldiers scattered around the world, looked at life through more sophisticated eyes. Former plantation workers used the GI Bill to obtain an education and enter the middle class. Meanwhile, a growing tide of Mainlanders (arriving on bigger and faster aircraft) came to Hawai'i to get away from it all. Fermenting changes within the community began to upset the older, quieter values and lifestyles.

One example of those changing values was supplied by the hippies, young wanderers who began to flock to Maui in the 1960s. They sought the warm shores of Lahaina, filled the crossroads village of Paia, and started religious colonies in Haiku. Their costumes and actions appeared outlandish to citizens of Maui who had only recently begun to enjoy the fruits of American middle-class prosperity. Some resented the free-and-easy way in which these young "coast haoles" helped themselves to the mangoes, bananas, guavas and avocados which they naively assumed were available free to all. Many of the newcomers were unwashed, wore their hair long, and dressed in rags.

But many had money to spend and others had food stamps, and the influx of new customers added to the growth or survival of many small village stores.

A nudist colony formed at the remote Big Beach at Makena, and Maui's vice squad began to arrest hippies for nude sunbathing. Mayor Cravalho appointed a Human Relations Council to consider the matter of how to deal with the strange newcomers. The county enforced sanitation laws and established an anti-hitch-hiking law.

One community on Maui became famous in the local news as the Banana Patch. A banana farmer in Peahi gave some of the "flower children" permission to camp out in his banana grove. A colony of treehouses and shacks grew in the secluded gulch.

In May 1970, authorities posted quarantine signs at the Banana Patch, thinking that a hepatitis epidemic had originated there. In fact, there was little hepatitis there, and when Patch owner David Joseph went to court, the judge ruled that the state had no legal authority to impose a quarantine.

A dysentery epidemic later in 1970 was a serious one, but though it also was blamed on the "young transients," epidemiological study found that the epidemic had been spread by a single batch of the Hawaiian staple food poi produced in Central Maui.

As the years went by, the hippies either assimilated into the Maui community or left the island. Maui continued to have a reputation for "magic" and to attract those looking for a spiritually based way of life.

But the hippies were not the only new immigrants of the sixties. A steady stream of middle-aged and older folks intent on retiring to a warm place came to look at Maui, often to buy an apartment in one of the condominiums springing up wherever they could get close to the Pacific shore. People with money to invest, who could afford a vacation home, were soon streaming in.

Speculation set in, and condominiums were bought one day and sold the next for profits of thousands. Condos began to sell so fast that the phenomenon arose of sales from blueprints. In 1978, people were standing in line a year ahead of construction to draw lots for the privilege of buying a one-bedroom apartment for $125,000. By 2001, the want ads included one-bedroom apartments for many times that amount.

Efforts during these years to discern the future for Hawai'i's economic development seemed to come up with one conclusion: tourism. It had been clear for some time that agriculture, while still the mainstay, could not provide the kind of future that would keep Maui's children at home. From 1940 to 1960, the county's population fell from 56,000 to 43,000.

With statehood, and the increase in air travel, county leaders saw an opportunity. Maui began its journey toward a reputation as "the best island in the world," a journey in which it would gain much but lose much as well.

KAʻANAPALI AND LAHAINA

American Factors Inc. (Amfac), owners of Pioneer Mill at Lahaina, also owned one of Maui's most desirable areas, a place called Kaʻanapali, four miles west of Lahaina. The company planners saw its potential as a super tourist resort, with near-perfect climate, uninterrupted miles of white sand beach and clear, calm waters. Surrounding sugar cane fields provided green open space and rose in upland sweeps to blue-green mountains. In addition to all this, there was the historic "lady with the past," old Lahaina with its memories of the aliʻi, the missionaries and the whalers.

There was one additional important advantage to the planning and development that followed–Kaʻanapali had a single owner. This enabled the development at Kaʻanapali of the state's first master-planned resort, a model of what a "destination resort" should be.

Over the next few decades, six luxury hotels, four condominiums, two golf courses and a shopping center were built along Kaʻanapali beach. The resort also attracted championship golf tournaments, launching Maui as a golf destination.

Simultaneously with the initial development of Kaʻanapali, Amfac cooperated with the new Lahaina Restoration Foundation and the county in the historic restoration of Lahaina. The house which had been occupied by missionary doctor Dwight Baldwin was restored and opened as a museum, and an old ship similar to a whaling vessel was anchored nearby and made into a small whaling museum. The county established the Lahaina Historic District and set architectural controls and height limits that would keep the town's historic profile intact.

The Lahaina Restoration Foundation has continued in its restoration of old buildings and sites in the area, including the old printing house on the Lahainaluna High School campus, Hale Paʻi.

In 1993, archaeologists dug into the softball field at Malu-ʻulu-o-Lele Park and found that the ancient island of Mokuʻula still lay buried there. This island and the fishpond which surrounded it served as a political and religious center from ancient times to the emergence of the Maui kingdom in the sixteenth century. The Friends of Mokuʻula formed to restore this site as a place where visitors and residents could experience Hawaiian traditions and learn the history of pre-contact Hawaiʻi.

Lahaina thrived as a tourist destination, with its quaint architecture and ocean views. Art became a major product, from the homegrown work of artists exhibiting under the banyan tree near the old Pioneer Inn to the slick commercial art sold in galleries on Front Street. The streets of old Lahaina were crowded at all seasons with thousands from around the world, seeking sun and fun.

KAPALUA

North of Lahaina, Maui Land & Pineapple Co. owned many acres of land that had been in pineapple and ranching. The company began planning a resort development in the 1960s.

This master-planned resort of 1,650 acres was to be surrounded by a working pineapple plantation, and many of the old plantation buildings were retained in the design. In 1975, the first golf course opened, followed three years later by the Kapalua Bay Hotel. The first increment of condominium apartments sold out in 1976 before they were built.

By the turn of the century, Kapalua included nearly 700 homes and condominiums, three championship golf courses, restaurants and shops, twenty tennis courts and two hotels.

The building of the Ritz-Carlton, Kapalua Hotel was delayed by the discovery of a massive ancient burial ground. Hundreds of burials were unearthed before public protests brought the digging to a halt. In February 1989, ML&P President Colin Cameron decided that the hotel must be relocated farther inland. The Honokahua burial site was restored as a perpetual resting place for what archeologists estimated could be as many as 2,000 human remains dating back as early as the fifth century.

This situation resulted in the statewide establishment of island burial councils that would monitor future situations in which development uncovered burials.

Kapalua and Maui Land & Pineapple Co. have been leaders in environmental conservation. In 1992, ML&P dedicated an 8,661-acre native forest at the summit of Pu'u Kukui above Kapalua as a private preserve in the care of The Nature Conservancy of Hawai'i. In 1996, Kapalua became the first resort in the world to be certified by Audubon International under the Audubon Heritage Program in recognition of the resort's care for the environment in its mountain-to-sea land holdings.

KIHEI

On the south side, development took a different route. As late as 1970, except for a couple of condominiums, there were no high-rise buildings, and Kihei Road wove through scenic views of the sea and a great sweep of Haleakala's western ramparts. Virgin beaches still stretched for miles from Ma'alaea out along Kihei's coast to Makena.

The south coast had been opened for development by the federally funded planning efforts of the late 1960s, which set up zoning for the entire coast. Water was the limiting factor. The county dealt with that by entering into a joint venture with several large property owners to construct the Central Maui water transmission line to serve the growing need from Kihei to Makena.

In a few short years, high-rise apartment hotels and condominiums, many looking more like foursquare penitentiary buildings than vacation resorts, crowded the shore. One writer described the skyline of Kihei as "a broken picket fence."

The dry, stony, lava-strewn hills above Kihei, where only the hardy kiawe tree once grew, became the abode of millionaires who built modern houses with picture windows framing spectacular views of Kahoʻolawe, Lanaʻi, and the broken skyline of Kihei below. The single road serving Kihei, now solid with condominiums, shopping centers, fast-food outlets and real estate offices, became jammed with traffic which seemed bumper-to-bumper at all hours.

The addition of the Piʻilani Highway, parallel to the old road and running out to the development at Wailea, temporarily lessened the traffic problems. But by the end of the century, even the highway often looked more like a parking lot, as long lines of cars inched along and motorists' frustration rose.

Kihei's rapid and often unsightly development was partly the result of there being many different land owners in Kihei, each with individual plans and profit motives, while county planners failed to hold the line against the runaway development. Kihei became the model for the wrong way to go about expansion.

WAILEA

At Wailea, on the other hand, Kaʻanapali-style planning produced a resort of world-class hotels in a manicured green landscape kept lush by the water from Central Maui.

In the 1960s, Alexander & Baldwin acquired the golden egg that would be called Wailea. Once grazing land for Ulupalakua Ranch, located just up the mountain, it consisted of 1,500 acres covered with a forest of spiny kiawe and festooned with a series of white sand beaches. It was served by one dusty dirt road, and the beaches were usually deserted.

In 1971 the Wailea Development Company was formed and began to turn the Wailea property into a first-class resort. It was to be a low-rise "City of Flowers" on a spectacular coastline. Over the next thirty years, Wailea developed five luxury hotels with more than 2,500 rooms, condominium complexes with more than 1,000 units, private homes, a shopping center, three golf courses, tennis courts and restaurants.

MAKENA

Not everyone was happy to see Maui turn into a vacation paradise. Environmentalists, Hawaiians and those who valued the small-town local lifestyle worried that the influx of strangers in rental cars and the construction of elaborate fantasy hotels on isolated beaches would ruin their island home.

The conflict played out in many ways. One of the most visible fights against development in the 1980s was between Hui Alanui O Makena and Seibu Hawai'i, Inc.

The Hui was born when Seibu traded the county some land at Big Beach for the 1,100-foot-long road parcel between its Maui Prince Hotel and Naupaka Beach. The company, citing county plans, wanted to remove the road to accommodate its resort development.

The Hui, made up of Native Hawaiians and their supporters, believed the shoreline road to be a segment of the historic Pi'ilani Trail that once circled Maui. Already, in the 1970s, the traditional shoreline road had been cut off at the entrance to Wailea to allow resort development direct access to the beach. A new road, Wailea Alanui, was routed through the resort area. Now, Seibu proposed to do something similar, creating a new, wide highway to replace the potholed dirt road along the shore.

Over the next couple of years, Hui Alanui O Makena filed several lawsuits against Seibu, the state and the county in its effort to stop the closure of the road. The conflict was resolved in 1987 through a mediation process in which former Mayor Elmer Cravalho was a key figure. Under the compromise reached, the road segment in front of the hotel would remain open as a 20-foot-wide stone-paved walkway. No vehicles would be allowed.

Among the items in the agreement were requirements for Seibu to pay $25,000 to the Hui for legal expenses, maintain the dirt road leading to Big Beach, create a public park on the south corner of Naupaka Beach and aid in the formation of a nonprofit corporation to preserve Hawaiian cultural heritage.

Though the loss of an intact shoreline road at Naupaka Beach bothered some, Hui kupuna Eddie Chang put an optimistic spin on the results: "We never lost the road. It's still alive. Only the cars lost the road," he said.

HANA

It was the road that was the attraction on the verdant coastline where the narrow winding Hana Highway, built in the 1920s, stretched from Central Maui to Hana. Residents strenuously opposed widening the road or the historic one-lane bridges across the many streams on East Maui's windward side. But Hana Highway was paved and improved enough that, by centuryís end, more than half a million visitors a year made it as far as the Kipahulu section of the Haleakala National Park.

While the increased visitor traffic kept the little town of Hana alive, the Hana Ranch and the Hotel Hana-Maui, built by financier Paul I. Fagan after World War II, struggled to remain profitable. Many Hana residents opened bed-and-breakfast establishments, grew exotic flowers, or made the long drive to Central Maui to earn a living.

CHAPTER 12

MAUI IN THE NEW MILLENNIUM:
1980 AND BEYOND

Mauians struggled during the last decades of the twentieth century to adapt to their new status as citizens of an island that had become a world-famous "paradise."

Maui's beauty and charm drew millions of visitors and thousands of new residents. In 1980 the island had just under 63,000 residents. By 1999, Maui's population totaled 112,197, and more than 43,000 tourists were on the island each day. Such rapid expansion created many growing pains.

Schools and sewage treatment plants ran over capacity, crime and drug use went up, and housing was scarce and expensive. Helicopters and jet skis disturbed nature's quiet. Newcomers to the island who had fled Mainland crowding and pollution clashed over development issues with kama'aina who remembered the days when the economy was so stagnant that their children could not find jobs.

The economic boom continued through the eighties, but the nineties were a different story. Like the rest of the state, Maui suffered when Japan's economy ran into trouble and spending by Japanese investors and visitors decreased. On Maui, hotel building had come to a halt, so high-paid construction workers left the island. All that remained of the great hotel-building frenzy, it seemed, were low-paid service jobs.

Once again, as they had looked for an alternative to agriculture back in the fifties, the county's leaders sought other industries, hoping to decrease dependence on tourism. In 1984, Maui Economic Development Board Chairman Colin Cameron described a new concept: a campus-like park where research and development projects could take place. The first buildings of the new Maui Research & Technology Park in Kihei opened in 1992. One tenant of the park would be the Maui High Performance Computing Center, home of a supercomputer ranked among the 100 most powerful supercomputers in the world, designed to support both military and private industry projects.

The Kihei center, along with "Science City" atop Haleakala, connected Maui to the world of high technology. Still, it was sometimes difficult to persuade high-tech companies that their kind of business belonged on an island better known for sun and surf.

Maui continued to attract the rich and famous, who enjoyed Maui's custom of politely ignoring celebrities in search of peace and privacy. A few of these made Maui their home and participated in community life.

And that life, while often hectic and demanding in ways earlier generations could not have imagined, was increasingly filled with rich cultural and recreational opportunities.

The Hawaiian language and culture underwent a renaissance statewide. One focus of that renaissance was the island of Kahoʻolawe, so close to Maui and considered a part of the county.

It was from Maui in 1976 that a group of people set out in boats for what would become the first illegal occupation of the island that had been a military target since 1941. After two days alone on the island, two Molokaʻi men, Walter Ritte and Noa Emmett Aluli, reached a spiritual turning point in their own lives that also marked a turning point for Hawaiʻi. The two would be among the leaders in the Protect Kahoʻolawe ʻOhana, whose goal was to stop the bombing and reclaim Kahoʻolawe.

Many years of efforts by the Protect Kahoʻolawe ʻOhana resulted in an end to the bombing in 1990. In 1994, the island was returned to the State of Hawaiʻi, and its restoration began. Maui became the base for the Kahoʻolawe Island Reserve Commission, with Aluli its first president.

Maui children began to learn Hawaiian language and culture in the Punana Leo O Maui Hawaiian immersion preschool in 1987. Some of these children continued their education in Hawaiian immersion classes in the public schools, young pioneers in the reestablishment of Hawaiian as a living language.

Canoe clubs and hula halau thrived as Mauians of all ethnic backgrounds sought to increase their understanding of the islands' host culture.

Western culture also blossomed on Maui.

Maui Community Theatre, active for decades, found a home in Wailuku's 'Iao Theater, built as a movie theater in 1928. Young thespians learned their craft at the Maui Youth Theatre (later the Maui Academy of Performing Arts) and Baldwin Theatre Guild. The vibrant Maui theatrical community produced performers whose fame spread far beyond Maui, such as Na Hoku Hanohano award-winning musicians Keali'i Reichel and Amy Hanaiali'i Gilliom, whose partner, Willie Kahaiali'i, also grew up on Maui.

Visual artists flourished on Maui as well, with the best of their work showing at the annual Art Maui juried exhibition.

All the arts found a home at the new Maui Arts & Cultural Center. The center opened in 1994, the product of years of planning by a corps of volunteers and of funding from the state and county governments and thousands of private donors. With a 1,200-seat theater aptly named "Castle" and high-quality surrounding facilities, the center showcased world-class entertainers from B.B. King to Mikhail Baryshnikov as well as films, community events and the best of island talent.

Paia became a windsurfing capital, drawing enthusiasts from all over the world to the famous surfing beach at Ho'okipa. The more daring and skilled took to the great storm surf at "Jaws," where jet skis towed surfers into place at the crest of giant waves crashing against a cliff near Haiku.

Professional sports attracted crowds and sent Maui's image worldwide by television coverage of events from golf tournaments on the resort courses to the Hula Bowl College all-star football games at Wailuku's War Memorial Stadium. And long-distance runners from around the world enjoyed spectacular views during races like the Hana Relays, Maui Marathon and the Run to the Sun up Mount Haleakala.

Services for people in need grew, with the establishment of shelters for battered women, abused children, recovering alcoholics and homeless families. The J. Walter Cameron Center, opened in Wailuku in 1973, was the successor to the Alexander House Settlement that had provided social services to Maui during the first half a century. The Cameron Center housed a collection on non-profit agencies.

The environment, threatened by development and pollution, had many defenders, and they enjoyed some victories. The crater at Haleakala had become easily accessible to the public when a new road to the summit opened in 1935, and the summit became the nation's 30th national park in 1961. The park later gained the unique Kipahulu Valley and the beautiful waterfalls and pools of 'Oheo Gulch.

Other vast areas of acreage were preserved through the efforts of The Nature Conservancy. These included 123 acres in Kipahulu which would serve as a buffer between the indigenous wildlife in the upper valley and the park with its thousands of visitors, and a 5,230-acre preserve at Waikamoi, on the slopes of Haleakala. The Conservancy also formed the state's first partnerships with groups of major landowners to protect watershed areas, taking on management of 100,000 acres near Waikamoi in 1991 and 47,000 acres on West Maui above Ka'anapali in 1998.

The efforts of many citizens, working as the "State Park at Makena," helped to purchase Big Beach from a private hui. The grass-roots movement to acquire what had been called "the crown jewel of Hawai'i's undeveloped beaches" began in the 1980s and finally succeeded in 1994 with the purchase of 145.3 acres.

As the century ended, Mauians believed their island was still one of the world's best places to live, despite its challenges. With its small-town charm combined with increased sophistication and the great variety of terrain and climate within a few short miles, it offered the possibility of a unique lifestyle. Like those in the rest of Hawai'i, Maui's people lived in interracial harmony. Their daily lives were carried out in a physical setting of great beauty.

True, the island was no longer the pristine natural setting its people enjoyed when Captain Cook first sailed into its waters – but then, neither did the people of the twenty-first century live in a society disrupted by its rulers' war or controlled by a strict kapu system.

Nor was Maui any longer the peaceful plantation society of pre-World War II times–but neither was it a virtual fiefdom ruled by an oligarchy and lacking in opportunity for the majority of its citizens.

Whatever its problems, many who visited or lived on the island of Maui as a new century began would agree that it still deserved its traditional motto:

Maui No Ka Oi. Maui is the best.

2000-2010
THE ECONOMY

Maui's population continued to grow—from 117,644 persons in 2000 to 144,372 by 2010—due more from natural increase than in-migration. Hispanics became ten (10) percent of the population, an increase that started when Maui Land & Pineapple Company ("ML&P") began to use Costa Rican workers in the 1980's.

Maui's popularity as a world famous vacation paradise continued with visitor arrivals reaching 2.3 million by 2012 versus 1.8 million in 2000. The average daily visitor census was 50,976 by 2012 compared to 41,819 in 2000. More visitors started to stay in time-share accommodations and vacation rentals. Hotel room rates and revenue per hotel room set new records. Several hotel resorts were sold to off-shore corporations.

Maui Land & Pineapple Company ("ML&P") shut down its pineapple operation, laying off hundreds of workers, to become a strictly land operation. Its Kapalua Resort and golf courses were sold off and a major housing development is planned above the West Maui airport at Mahinahina.

Former ML&P executives began Halimaile Pineapple, concentrating on growing premium fresh fruit on 1,000 acres of former ML&P lands and employing about 200 former ML&P workers.

Hawaiian Commerical & Sugar Company ("HC&S") remains the only sugar cane plantation still operating in Hawai'i. Advances in processing sugar cane as a biofuel are a key research area for the company. The majority of HC&S sugar is shipped to Crocket, California for final refining to be sold under the C&H Sugar label.

Haleakalā and 'Ulupalakua Ranches created the Maui Cattle Co. to process and sell local beef.

The Maui News was sold by the Cameron family to Ogdon Newspapers, a mainland daily newspaper chain, based in Wheeling, West Virginia, which took over publication on January 1, 2000.

The economy in Maui's rural areas rebounded when about 500 bed and breakfast ("B&B") and transient rentals reopened. Some 800 to 1,000 "illegal" B&B and transient rentals had been closed, impacting jobs, small stores and restaurants particularly around Ha'ikū and Hāna. The County finally instituted a reasonable permitting system, but capped the number of B&Bs, ag-tourism units and transient rentals.

The building of retail centers and the addition of big box stores was the major source of employment gains. Alexander & Baldwin sold a 24-acre Kahului parcel for development of a Target store.

Two big wind farms built on the slopes above Mā'alaea and above Mākena now sell about ninety (90) percent of their wind-energy to Maui Electric. Future sites are being considered for the Kaupō, Kahikinui, Kapalua, and the Pā'ia-Ha'ikū areas.

Farmers markets proliferated and upscale restaurants began to feature local produce.

CONSERVATION/ENVIRONMENT

Hawaiian Commercial & Sugar Company ("HC&S") began meeting with community groups in Pu'unene in an effort to resolve questions about the effects of burning sugar cane fields. Updates on when burning is scheduled are posted online by HC&S. Any burning ban would severely impact sugar's future on Maui.

Johnny Baldwin donated several thousand acres of Kīpahulu to Haleakalā National Park while 'Ulupalakua Ranch dedicated thousands of acres above Kīhei to prevent development. Land around Honolua Bay was put into conservation through the efforts of the Save Honolua Bay Organization. West side reef studies are being made in connection with an ongoing dispute concerning the County's sewage disposal polluting the ocean. Maui's reefs are an important draw for visitors wanting to snorkel. Federal environmental grants have been obtained to help maintain sections of the coastline.

Shark attacks became more common. The State began a long-term study involving tagging sharks to discover why Maui's waters are seeing more sharks. Possibilities include the increased green sea turtle population (a favorite food of sharks) and more people in the water, many unaware of ocean hazards.

There is concern about tourists being sometimes insensitive to the environment, particularly sections of the 'Ahihi-Kina'u Natural area as well as private property around pools and waterfalls in East Maui.

Non-residents coming in to fish and gather 'opihi in Hāna area was also a concern.

Downhill bicycle commercial operations continue to operate along Haleakalā Highway. Local residents object to the slowing of traffic by the bike rides.

Officials at Haleakalā National Park are planning, over the next 10 to 15 years, to reduce the number of visitors brought by commercial tour operators to the park.

CULTURE

The Celestial Cinema is a big draw at the Maui Film Festival, a popular outdoor, very glitzy show at a Wailea golf course that ties in with celebrity events.

The annual Halloween Lahaina event (once called the Mardi Gras of the Pacific) was allowed to continue. It is now tightly controlled to prevent public lewdness and offending Hawaiian sensibilities through the efforts of the Lahaina Town Action Committee, which helps organize and run the event while the County handles permits.

The Kapalua Ritz-Carlton established an annual three-day, authentic Hawaiian cultural event in May called Celebration of the Arts with workshops, performances and Hawaiian crafts.

Within the Hawaiian population, the ongoing pro-Akaka and sovereignty dispute was still a major concern. Hawaiian Language immersion schools continued to gain in popularity.

More Hawaiians are living in Kula due to the new 400-lot Hawaiian Homes subdivision in adjacent Waiohuli. The Waiohuli Hawaiian Homestead Association is leading in constructing the Waiohuli Community and Recreation Center.

While the aloha spirit prevails on Maui, the influx of more outsiders is endangering it. Mauians are aware of and friendly toward others, willing to help without being asked. Many newcomers are not concerned about island ways and traditions. Some replicate California-like compounds, as evidenced by walled houses in much of Wailea and Makenā. As Maui receives more people from outside of Hawaiʻi, this will remain an issue.

A NOTE ON SOURCES

Research, specifically for this book, began in Honolulu in 1973 and consisted at first of general readings in Pacific and Hawaiian history, which led to a particular interest in Captain Cook and the Third Voyage. Returning to Maui in 1975, renewed interest in local history led to sources on Maui itself and especially to the Hawaiian Room at the Kahului Library, which has a good collection of books, periodicals, and documents. A rare find there is a copy of the original publication, *Voyage to the Pacific Ocean, 1776-1780*, three volumes published in London in 1784 and containing the journal kept first by Cook and later, after his death, by Lieutenant James King. Volume II contains William Bligh's drawing of the island made as the ships lay off Kahului in November 1778. Some of the sources were found at the Wailuku and Lahaina public libraries and at the library of Maui Community College.

A course on the history of Maui given for Chaminade College helped in gathering data, especially as field trips to historic sites were used to supplement the written materials.

The Bishop Museum Library contains rich resources for the historian, although separate catalog listings for Maui are not extensive. The Honolulu Academy of Arts has photographs available at small cost, and there are, besides, the fine collection of documents and photographs of old prints and drawings available from the Archives of Hawai'i.

Visits and searches were conducted in the summers of 1977 and 1978 in England in the British Museum (General) Library and the Manuscript Library; in the Museum of Natural History, where the watercolors of William Ellis (Third Voyage) are found; and especially the Admiralty series of the Public Record Office, London (PRO), where the original logs and journals of the *Resolution* and *Discovery* are found. The Museum of Mankind in Burlington Gardens, a part of the British Museum, has a very fine collection of Hawaiian art on exhibition. This contains some beautiful pieces such as feather cloaks and helmets (on loan from the British Royal Family), carvings, and other artifacts from the voyages of Cook, Portlock and Dixon, Vancouver, Byron and others.

The British Museum "store," or storeroom, outside London contains over a thousand Hawaiian items from which approximately 300 were selected by anthropologist Adrienne Kaeppler for the Cook Bicentennial Exhibit (1978) at the Bishop Museum. It was disappointing to find that the artists, Webber and Ellis, the former having done the best known and earliest drawings and paintings of Hawai'i, apparently did not make sketches while the ships cruised and traded off Maui, November 26,30, 1778. This makes Bligh's drawing of the island unique.

Several weeks in the summer of 1978 were spent in further research in the British Museum Library, the National Maritime Museum at Greenwich, and the Maritime Museums of Hull and Whitby where many of the logs of English whalers were examined and some new material on Captain Cook was found. The logs of Vancouver's voyage were consulted in the new Public Records facility at Kew where automation has speeded the process of research to a matter of minutes instead of the hours required in the old facility at Chancery Lane.

Logs of twelve whale ships in the Peabody Museum of Salem, Massachusetts, were read for Maui references and the log of the ship Massachusetts yielded the most detailed description of the Olowalu Massacre. The museum's library has a separate category for Maui in its card catalog. The references are under the heading spelled in the old form, "Mowee."

The small collection of books and documents in the Museum at Wailuku (Maui Historical Society) includes the remarkable notebooks of Elspeth Sterling containing information or listings of important historic sites on Maui. The historical files maintained by Inez Ashdown in the Planning Office in the County Building proved valuable.

Finally, there is the material stored above the office of the Lahaina Restoration Foundation. The material, though not catalogued, is not difficult to use and consists of boxes approximately eight inches square labeled simply, "Lahaina, general,"

"Missionaries," "Hawaiians," etc. containing quotes from general publications, periodicals, diaries, journals and logs, neatly typed on 5 x 8 sheets. Many of these typescripts have been copied from originals or secondary sources in the Library of the Hawaiian Mission Children's Society in Honolulu. There is a wealth of material there for the researcher willing to dig in and, added to the excellent study of the Seamen's Hospital that the Frosts did for the Restoration, *Rendezvous in Lahaina,* this is probably the richest and most concentrated resource on Maui's history to be found.

Company records, annual reports, the Wailuku Sugar Company's history, Centennial 1862-1962, the local newspapers, taped interviews, the Mayor's Bicentennial Report (1976) and the 1977 report were sources for valuable material for this history of the Island of Maui.

References for individual chapters are listed in the section following the Basic References.

BASIC REFERENCES
BIBLIOGRAPHY

General Histories, Logs, and Journals

Alexander, W. D., *Brief History of the Hawaiian People,* American Book, 1899.

Alexander & Baldwin, Inc. 1999 Annual Report

Anderson, Bern, *Surveyor of the Sea, The Life and Voyages of Captain George Vancouver,* University of Washington Press, Seattle, 1960.

Arago, Jacques, *Narrative of a Voyage Round the World* during the years 1817-18-19, and 20, London, 1823.

Ashdown, Inez, *Ke Alaloa O Maui, The Broad Highway of Maui,* Wailuku, Hawai'i, 1971.

Atlas of Hawaii, University Press of Hawai'i, 1973.

Barrow, Tui Terrance, *Captain Cook in Hawaii,* Island Heritage, Honolulu, 1976.

Beaglehole, J. C., *The Journals of Captain James Cook,* Volume III in two parts "The Voyage of the *Resolution* and *Discovery,* 1776-1780," Hakluyt Society, Cambridge, 1955-69.

————, *The Life of Captain James Cook,* Stanford University Press, 1974.

Bingham, Hiram, *A Residence of Twenty-One Years in the Sandwich Islands,* Praeger, N. Y., 1969.

Bird, Isabella L., *Six Months in the Sandwich Islands,* (1873) University of Hawai'i Press, Honolulu, 1964.

British Public Record Office, Admiralty 51, #4557, Log of HMS *Discovery,* #4558 Cook's log of *Resolution* by William Langon; *Discovery* log by William Shuttleworth, Midshipman, Admiralty 55/26 master's log HMS *Discovery,* 1790-94 by Harry Humphreys contains handsome drawings by Humphreys who was midshipman, master's mate and finally master of Vancouver's ship *Discovery,* Admiralty 52 #4054 is the log of the *Blonde,* June 10, 1824 to Dec. 15, 1826.

Buck, Sir Peter H., *Explorers of the Pacific,* Bishop Museum, Honolulu, 1953.

Byron, George Anson Baron, *Voyage of HMS Blonde, to the Sandwich Islands in the Years 1824-25,* London, 1826. This volume was missing from the Library of the British Museum in 1978.

Campbell, Archibald, *A Voyage Round the World from 1806 to 1812,* facsimile reproduction of the Third American Edition of 1822. University of Hawai'i Press, Honolulu, 1967.

Campbell, Kimo, *Kaulana na Pua.*

Cheever, Rev. Henry T., *Life in the Sandwich Islands, or The Heart of the Pacific, as it was and is.* Barnes, New York, 1851.

Coffman, Tom, *Catch a Wave, Hawaii's New Politics,* Honolulu, 1972.

Cook, James, *A Voyage to the Pacific Ocean,* London, 1776-1780, N. Hughs, London 1784. Volumes I & II by Cook: Volume III by Capt. James King.

Crowningburg-Amalu, Samuel, *Jack Burns, A Portrait in Transition,* Mamalahoa Foundation, Honolulu, 1974.

Daws, Gavan, *Shoal of Time, A History of the Hawaiian Islands,* University Press of Hawai'i, 1968.

Day, A. Grove, *Hawai'i and Its People,* Meredith, N. Y., 1968.

Dibble, S., *History of the Sandwich Islands,* Lahainaluna, 1843.

Dodge, Ernest S., *Beyond the Capes, Pacific Exploration from Captain Cook to the Challenger* (1776-1877), Little, Brown, Boston, 1971.

————, *New England and the South Seas,* Harvard University Press, Cambridge, Mass., 1965.

Ellis, William, *Journal of William Ellis, Narrative of a Tour of Hawaii,* reprint of the London 1827 edition and the Hawai'i 1917 edition, Advertiser Publishing Co., Ltd. Honolulu, 1963.

Engledow, Jill and Sanford, Mary Cameron, *The Maui News,* "100 Years as Maui's Newspaper," Maui Publishing Co.: Wailuku, Hawaii (2000).

Fornander, Abraham, *An Account of the Polynesian Race, Its Origins and Migrations and the Ancient History of the Hawaiian People to the Times of Kamehameha I.*
Three volumes in one, Charles E. Tuttle, Rutland, Vermont, 1969.

————, *Antiquities,* Bishop Museum Memoirs, Fornander Collection of Hawaiian Antiquities and Folklore, Bishop Museum Press, Memoirs Volumes 4, 5 and 6, Honolulu, 1916-1917.

Frost and Frost, *Rendezvous in Lahaina,* A Study and Report on Seaman's Hospital, Lahaina Restoration Foundation, 1975.

Gowan, Rev. H. H., *The Paradise of the Pacific, Sketches of Hawaiian*

Scenery and Life, Skeffington and Son, London, 1892. Sept. 1886-June 1889.

Grenfell, Price A., *The Explorations of Captain James Cook in the Pacific,* Dover Publications, New York, 1971.

Hawai'i, State of, Department of Planning and Economic Development, Tourism in Hawai'i, Volume I, Honolulu, 1972.

Hawaiian Journal of History, Hawaiian Historical Society, Honolulu. Hopkins, Manley, Hawai'i, London, 1862.

Ii, John Papa, *Fragments of Hawaiian History,* Bishop Museum Press, Honolulu, 1973.

Jarves, J., *History of the Sandwich Islands,* London, 1843.

Judd, Gerrit P., *Hawaii, An Informal History,* Collier Books, New York, 1961.

Kamakau, Samuel M., *Ruling Chiefs of Hawaii,* The Kamehameha School Press, Honolulu, 1961, and *Index* to Ruling Chiefs compiled by E. P. Sterling, Bishop Museum, 1974. The Index is essential in using Kamakau. We have followed throughout spelling of Hawaiian names in the Index. On p. 83, Sterling quotes Stokes regarding the unreliability of Kamakau's dates and the fact that they were not accepted by his native contemporaries.

Kuykendall, Ralph S., *The Hawaiian Kingdom,* Three Volumes, University of Hawai'i Press, Honolulu, 1967.

Lahaina Restoration Foundation, Missionary Records and Notes from journals, letters, and published works referring to Maui and especially Lahaina history.

Ledyard, John, *Journal of Captain Cook's Last Voyage,* Oregon State, 1963.

Lind, Andrew W., *Hawaii's People,* third edition, University of Hawai'i Press, Honolulu, 1967.

Liziansky, Urey, *A Voyage Round the World* in the years 1803, 04, 05 and 06. Booth, London 1814. Facsimile published by Da Capo Press, New York, 1968.

Lloyd, Christopher, *Pacific Horizons,* London, 1977.

MacDonald, Alexander, *Revolt in Paradise,* Daye, New York, 1944.

Malo, David, *Hawaiian Antiquities,* Bishop Museum Press, Honolulu, 1976.

Maui Land & Pineapple Company, Inc. 1999 Annual Report.

Morrow, A. C. and Jack, Maui, *A Few Facts About the Valley Isle,* 1920. Portlock and Dixon, *Voyage Round the World.*

Ramil, Antonio V., Kalai'aina, County of Maui, Anvil-Maui Press: Wailuku, Hawai'i (1984).

Rydell, Raymond A., *Cape Horn to the Pacific,* Berkeley, 1952.

Samwell, David, *A Narrative of the Death of Captain James Cook,* in Hawaiian Historical Society reprints, #2.

Schoofs, Rev. Robert, ss.cc., *Pioneers of the Faith,* History of the Catholic Mission in Hawai'i (1827-1940). Revised by Fay Wren Midkiff, Edited and Published by Louis Boeynaems, ss.cc., Honolulu, 1978.

Shirey, Orville C., *Americans,* The Story of the 442nd Combat Team, Infantry Journal Press, Washington, 1947.

Simpich, Frederick, *Anatomy of Hawaii,* Coward McCann, New York, 1971.

Simpson, Sir George, *Narrative of a Journey Round the World, 1841-1842,* London, 1847.

Sinclair, Marjorie, *Nahi-'ena-'ena,* University Press, Honolulu, 1976.

Smith, Bradford, *Yankees in Paradise,* Lippincott, New York, 1956.

Starbuck, Alexander, *History of the American Whale Fishery,* vols. 1 and 2, Argosy Antiquarian, New York, 1964.

Stearns, Harold T., *Geology of the State of Hawaii,* Pacific Books, Palo Alto, 1966.

Steegmuller, Francis, *The Two Lives of James Jackson Jarves,* Part one, Yale University Press, New Haven, 1951.

Stewart, Charles, *Journal of a Residence in the Sandwich Islands, 1823-1825,* University of Hawai'i Press, Honolulu, 1970.

Strauss, W. Patrick, *Americans in Polynesia, 1783-1842,* Michigan State, E. Lansing, 1963.

Valentin, Francois, *Voyages and Adventures of La Pérouse,* from the fourteenth edition of the F. Valentin Abridgement, Tours 1875, University of Hawai'i Press, Honolulu, 1969.

Vancouver, George, *Voyage of Discovery to the North Pacific Ocean and Round the World,* Amsterdam, N. Israel; New York, Da Capo, 1968, 3 volumes. Reprint of the London edition of 1798.

Wenkam, Robert, *Maui, The Last Hawaiian Place,* Friends of the Earth, San Francisco, 1970.

CHAPTER SOURCES

CHAPTER 1

Most of the material for this chapter can be found in general histories of Hawai'i, among which Kuykendall, Kamakau, Fornander and Daws were most useful. Kuykendall's first chapter in Volume I called "A Glimpse of Ancient Hawaii," gives brief but excellent insight into the lives of the pre-contact Hawaiians.

My main sources on Maui, The Demigod are Luomala, K., *Maui-of-a-thousand tricks:* his oceanic and European biographers, Bishop Museum Bulletin "The Irresistible Maui," Honolulu 1949; Robert Wenkam, *Maui: The Last Hawaiian Place,* San Francisco, 1970, who gives a version of the story with several twists typical of Hawaiian humor; and Inez Ash-down, whose version comes straight from the older Hawaiian people of the Island who talk like it really did happen that way and not so very long ago at that. In the Ashdown version, Maui learned to make a fishing net, traveled the zigzag trail into the crater, then climbed the highest of the seven cones, or peaks, where he snared great La, the Sun, and advised him to travel more slowly. La agreed to do this for six months of the year and Maui released him. Thus, the Ko'olau gap was named after the fish net (ko-olau) and the Hele-mau Trail (zigzag trail) means Maui traveled steadfastly. People mistakenly call the trail Hale-mau'u, meaning grass house, which makes no sense at all. Place names in Hawaiian were a way of telling a story like this "to make sense and to have a moral. Translate the place names correctly and the story is told so." (Ashdown to author, January 1978.)

For the geological formation of the island, I used Harold T. Stearns, *Geology of the State of Hawaii,* Pacific Books, Palo Alto, 1966. A lyrical description of the island as it would be seen from the air makes a fine introduction to his main section, Chapter 7, pages 151-165.

For the Polynesians and their settlements in the Islands, I used Fornander, the general histories, and had the benefit of several talk-sessions with Dr. Kenneth Emory, Senior Anthropologist, Bishop Museum, whose report, "Endangered Hawaiian

Archaeological Sites Within Maui County," February 1979, Report 79-2, Bishop Museum, Honolulu, was also helpful.

Herb Kawainui Kane and his book, *Voyage,* Island Heritage, Honolulu, 1976, as well as his article and paintings under the title of "The Pathfinders," in *National Geographic,* Vol. 146, No. 6, Dec. 1974, gave good background on the great Polynesian voyagers.

The story of the Piʻilani ruling chiefs of Maui is condensed from the first two chapters of Kamakau. It may serve to give some hint as to the dynastic system of ruling families and as a preface to the next chapter which tells how another strong family of chiefs came to dominate the island of Maui and through their descendants, to play an important role in the formation and development of a true Hawaiian Kingdom.

CHAPTER 2

For this chapter, I relied mainly on Kamakau's *Ruling Chiefs of Hawaiʻi.* In addition, I found the series of newspaper articles "The Story of Maui Royalty' by Sammy Crowningburg-Amalu quite useful for references though like Kamakau it is based on oral sources and should be used with caution.

For bringing this source to my attention, I am indebted to June Gutmanis who gave me copies of her clippings of the articles from the Honolulu *Advertiser.* These appeared in a series of 53 articles between April and June 1956 under the pseudonym Kapiikauinamoku.

Volume II of Fornander's *Origins of the Polynesian People* was also a source for Chapter 2.

CHAPTER 3

My main sources for the pre-Cook Spanish contacts with the Hawaiian Islands are the journals of La Pérouse, and Dr. Rollin, Surgeon with the French Expedition, Vancouver, and those of Cook and members of his Third Voyage, especially James Burney.

The most important source I found for early accounts by Hawaiians was the narrative and journal of the English missionary, William Ellis. Ellis followed up on clues he found in talking to chiefs and others on Hawai'i in 1822. Hawaiian accounts of a white priest, Pa'ao, who landed at Kohala on Hawai'i perhaps a hundred years before Cook are found in several sources of which Ellis' is one of the best.

There are several versions of the landing of a boat at Kealakekua Bay without a sail but covered with a canopy of hides or white tapa. Seven white men were said to have arrived in the boat. They went up into the mountains where they dwelt for a time. They were described in one version as departing from the bay in their boat, not to be seen again. While they lived in Hawai'i, Opili, the son of Pa'ao, also a powerful priest, was sent to communicate with these men and was able to do so because he knew their language. Another version tells of these white men settling in Hawai'i and marrying Hawaiian women. There are still some Hawaiians who claim descent from them.

Ellis was told that the principal person among the white men was called Manahini. This is a Polynesian word for stranger, visitor, or guest. In modern Hawaiian, the word is spelled Malahini. (Ellis, page 318.)

The tradition of a Spanish shipwreck on the coast of Maui is still strong among the Hawaiians. The chief who crossed his fingers and pointed to the land when the officers on the *Discovery* admired his iron dagger, may have been trying to describe an anchor rather than a cross, though the cross is the usual interpretation. John Young, the adviser of Kamehameha the First, who arrived at Kona in 1786 and lived the rest of his life in Hawai'i, once spoke of a large iron anchor that had been sitting on Maui for many years before Cook's arrival. One of the chiefs on Hawai'i told Ellis that there was a tradition of a ship having touched at Maui prior to Cook's arrival. Other natives denied the story (p. 319).

The reference to iron daggers observed off Maui on November 27, 1778 is from the Journal of James Burney taken from a typescript copy in the Bishop Museum: "The chiefs had two long pieces of iron shaped like skewers, well painted which we supposed to have been got from the Spaniards. One of the Indians held his 2 forefingers across each other and pointed to the land which we construed into the Spaniards having set up a cross on shore. These circumstances however fell far short of a proof."

In any case, I believe that the Spanish knew the islands were here but, for some unknown reason, kept that knowledge secret. The most convincing evidence is the Spanish map which Cook, La Pérouse, and Vancouver had available on their voyages and the general belief on the part of both the latter as they explored the area of the map, that the Los Majos islands of the Spanish map were, in fact, the windward islands of Hawai'i.

The map* shown in the plates is from the collection of my friend, Darrell Nielson, who purchased it in Paris in 1970. Though the map may have been published later, it appears to be a facsimile of an earlier Spanish map. The date on the map is 1587, nearly thirty years after Juan Gaetano is supposed to have discovered the Los Majos Islands, and 181 years *before* Cook. One hundred and eighty-one years is a long time, long enough for all memory of the Spanish ships to be forgotten by the Hawaiians; long enough for the secret knowledge of the discovery to have been forgotten or lost by the Spanish.

I do not doubt that the truth of the matter will become known as research continues. Discussion of the theory of Spanish discovery is found in practically every work on the Hawaiian Islands. One of the most interesting of these is found in the Bern Anderson book on the life and voyages of Capt. George Vancouver, *Surveyor of the Sea.*

The Cook journals are, naturally, the most important sources for Chapter 3, along with Prof. Beaglehole's *Life of Captain James Cook.* The journal of David Samwell, Surgeon's mate on board H.M.S. *Discovery* is my source for the visit of Ka-hekili to the ship on November 27, 1778.

Cook's own descriptions of the meetings with the Maui people are quoted from the publication of 1784, *Voyage to the Pacific Ocean 1776-1780,* listed under Basic References.

The description of the events at Kealakekua Bay and Cook's death is a composite of many accounts, among them, those of King, Burney, Ledyard, Samwell, and others. The nineteenth century

*This plate does not appear in this edition.

accounts of the Congregational missionaries were studied along with the accounts of modern historians including especially Kuykendall, Daws, Barrow, and Beaglehole.

Ledyard, Gore, and five others of the Cook Expedition, were undoubtedly the first Americans to visit Hawai'i.

Kamakau, who was strongly under the influence of the missionaries, appears to have followed the version of Cook's death which appeared in Dibble's *History* (1843) and since discredited. The missionary version was that Cook "was not a properly devout Christian but a presumptuous worm who accepted the worship of ignorant savages at the same time he infected them with venereal disease, and for this the true God struck him down." (Daws, p. 25) (Kamakau, pp. 92-104)

Villiers wrote that research among the Hawaiians while witnesses were still living showed that Cook was received as a great white chief. He suffered the priestly mumbo-jumbo which was a part of the Polynesian way of life in which all priests and chiefs seemed to be accepted as descended from the gods. Cook put up with it in the interest of good relations, and for the welfare of his crews. "He had done that before. It was the only sensible policy."

There is no question Cook was regarded as a high chief with divine Lono powers. Even after death, his body was treated as that of a high chief with powerful *mana.*

Another interesting footnote to the visit of King Ka-lani-'o-pu'u to Cook's flagship is found in Fornander's *Origins.* He cites Hawaiian accounts to the effect that the Hawaiian chief went aboard the *Resolution* off Wailua in the Ko'olau District. Ka-lani-'o-pu'u was in that area at the time but no Hawaiian account mentions that he went aboard personally, according to Fornander. However, he says that all accounts concur that Kamehameha went aboard and passed the night on the ship. These accounts describe a great wailing when Kamehameha did not return that night (November 30, 1778) as it was believed that he had been abducted. There was great rejoicing when he returned the next day.

Local tradition at Wailua-Keanae has it that it was from here that Cook's ships were first sighted. This is probably the case as the ships approached the Maui coast near there, then turned west to the Kahului area on the second day.

Further arguments for the Spanish theory are found in Sir George Simpson's *Narrative,* published in London in 1847. He believed the high and most southerly of the islands, Hawai'i, was most likely to have attracted the attention of the Spanish voyagers and that La Mesa on the old chart "no doubt describes Mauna Loa."

CHAPTER 4

As with the three previous chapters, the "backbone" for this chapter on the final battles is provided by Kamakau, and Daws. The sources for the Olowalu Massacre are Janion, Aubrey, *The Olowalu Massacre and Other Stories,* Heritage Press, Honolulu, 1976; the Xerox copy of the article from the Boston newspaper *Columbian Sentinel,* in the Bishop Museum; the Journal of Vancouver, and the log of the whaleship *Massachusetts.* Accounts of the massacre are included in all the general histories, and many of the missionary and 19th century visitors' journals. The blind injustice and cruelty of Captain Metcalf's massacre of innocent people on the coast of Maui in 1786 is a deplorable blot on the history of the early relations of Hawai'i and the United States.

I have tried to simplify as much as possible the complicated succession of battles between Kamehameha and Ka-hekili which ended with the battle of Nu'uanu. The details are to be found in every history of Hawai'i from Kamakau to Daws.

Fornander and Kamakau both wrote extensively on the reign of Ka-hekili. It is interesting to compare their accounts with those of Samwell, the first foreigner (haole) to describe this durable Hawaiian king, and Captains Nathaniel Portlock and George Vancouver, who knew Ka-hekili well in his last years. The English descriptions antedate Kamakau by half a century and were written with only the slightest background on the Hawaiians and their society.

I have drawn on Kamakau's Chapter XIII "Last Days of Ka-hekili," though modifying in this account Kamakau's tendency to emphasize the most gory details of the battles of the chiefs. One instance of this is his description of the disposition of the slain

Hawaiian chiefs and their warriors after Ka-hekili defeated them at Hana. The corpses were burned in the *imus* (ovens) below the Kau'iki fortress. This treatment was not necessarily considered savage or cruel. It was part of the practice of honorable disposal of the bodies of slain chiefs. As has been pointed out, the same "honors" were paid to Cook's body at Kealakekua Bay. The burning of bodies after battle may also have been practiced for sanitary reasons.

CHAPTER 5

The journals of Vancouver, Portlock, and Dixon are available in the Kahului Library where I consulted them for Chapter 5. These volumes are facsimile reproductions of the originals published in the late eighteenth century.

The exploits of La Pérouse were ignored by American writers in the nineteenth century and not until 1959 was he given proper notice in the form of two American books of exploration: Charles N. Rudkin, *The First French Expedition to California: La Pérouse in 1786,* Glen Dawson, Los Angeles, 1959 and Edward W. Allen, *The Vanishing Frenchman: The Mysterious Disappearance of La Pérouse* (Tuttle, Rutland, Vt., 1959).

Since then, the University Press of Hawai'i has published a translation of an abridged version of La Pérouse's report: *Voyages and Adventures of La Pérouse* from the fourteenth edition of the F. Valentin Abridgement, Tours 1875, translated by Julius S. Gassner, University of Hawai'i Press, 1969.

The translator points out several reasons for the lack of attention paid to La Pérouse in our histories. The original report was in French, published in Paris in 1797, and despite a number of translations in English (including one American edition published in Boston in 1801), the literature on La Pérouse was mostly in French and received scant notice in the United States. Another factor was the French Revolution and the fall of Louis XVI who had ordered the expedition. The wars of Napoleon followed and the news of La Pérouse was eclipsed by events.

Finally, though the discoveries of La Pérouse and his scientists aboard the French frigates, *Boussole* and *Astrolabe,* were of some importance to the opening of the Pacific, particularly their acute observations of the peoples visited in the Pacific lands (some of the journals read like modern anthropological research), the Admiral, his two ships, his officers and men disappeared into the Pacific without a trace. None survived to tell the tale, and it was forty years after the expedition left Botany Bay in Australia, that the fate of the French explorers was at last discovered.

Fortunately, the journals of the voyage were not lost. The French Admiral sent them back to France, first by de Lesseps overland from Kamchatka, and again, just before he disappeared, by the English Commodore Phillip, who delivered the documents from Australia to Paris.

The journals included the diaries of his officers, in particular the journal of the ship's surgeon, Dr. Rollin, which is a valuable supplement to that of La Pérouse. The expedition included some of France's most capable scientists, men of the Enlightenment, and their journals are among the most interesting to be found in the annals of the Pacific.

Vancouver's death and the appearance of his journals were sadly neglected in Britain and abroad. The Napoleonic Wars occupied the British for seventeen years after his death. However, the main reason for Vancouver's unwarranted neglect as a naval commander, explorer, and navigator, was due to the so-called "Camelford Affair." This affair was dragged through the press and the courts and involved an accusation by the young Lord Camelford, who was of the noble Pitt family.

This man accused Captain Vancouver of having him flogged during his service under Vancouver as a midshipman. These men, though not officers, were candidates for officer rank and flogging of midshipmen was not countenanced in the British Navy. The high family connections and the ferocity of Camelford's attack undoubtedly hurt Vancouver's reputation. A cartoon of the time illustrating a physical attack on Capt. Vancouver by the young English lord on a London street, added to Vancouver's near disgrace as it depicted him as a coward cringing from the blows of Lord Camelford's cane.

This affair embittered the last years of Vancouver's life and probably hastened his death as he was already a seriously ill man at the time. For more on Vancouver and the assessment of his life, see Bern Anderson, *Surveyor of the Sea, The Life and Voyages of Captain George Vancouver,* University of Washington Press, Seattle, 1960. Chapter 9 "The Islands of Los Majos" is one of the most persuasive arguments in support of the theory of an earlier discovery of Hawai'i by the Spanish. Reading these journals one cannot help but gain respect for Vancouver himself, but also for Kamehameha and the Maui King Ka-hekili, about whom there is very interesting material.

In Vancouver's journal, he describes a visit by Ka-hekili and his retinue off Waikiki. During this visit, night came on rather quickly and the surf was so high on the shore that Ka-hekili asked permission to stay on board *Discovery* overnight. Vancouver had a policy of no overnight visitors while in the Islands, but made an exception for the King on this particular night.

The captain then provided a fireworks display on board and tells in his log that the chiefs kept him awake talking most of the night about the fireworks. When Vancouver arose, he found the brother, Ka-'eo, still aboard but Ka-hekili had "jumped ship" at an early hour without ceremony. Ka-'eo apologized for his brother's hasty departure but Vancouver was apparently put out and wrote that he was "apprehensive that some accidental offense had been given him." Ka-'eo assured the captain "of the contrary and that such was his common practice of retiring." (Vancouver, Voyage of Discovery, II, 199.)

Nothing further is said by Vancouver about this incident. However, Menzies, botanist with the expedition, describes a harrowing scene which records the reason for Ka-hekili's sudden departure. Vancouver flew into such a rage over a most trivial matter, so frightening the king that he dashed into Menzie's cabin and "instantly jumping into his canoe through the port hole, paddled to the shore and saw no more of him." (Menzies *Journal,* p. 561, as quoted in Anderson, *Op. cit.* p. 148.)

This story compares with that of Captain Portlock who describes Ka-hekili off Waikiki jumping overboard in a high sea and recovering his canoe. The year was 1794 in both cases and

Ka-hekili, the cliff leaper, was considered to be sixty by Vancouver and as much as eighty-seven by Kamakau.

Ka-hekili must have been one of those remarkably strong Hawaiian chiefs who had constitutions of iron and who managed to survive the most dangerous vicissitudes of the Hawaiian wars.

The sport of *lelekawa* (cliff leaping) seems to have kept Ka-hekili in good shape. He had several favorite leaping cliffs on Maui: Kahakuloa was one; another the cliff called Pali Ka-hekili at Keanae, where local tradition has it the king injured his genitals so that he could no longer father children. Nevertheless, Vancouver was introduced to a son of Ka-hekili at Maui in 1794, whose age he judged to be fifteen. This would have made Ka-hekili seventy-two at the time of this son's birth. There is a large black stone below the Pali Ka-hekili at Keanae and its name is Pohaku-ule-o-Ka-hekili, or freely translated, "The stone of Ka-hekili's penis."

Local Maui tradition tells of at least one famous leap by this rugged king from the dangerous burial cliff at Keka'a Point, the cliff now occupied by the Hotel Sheraton-Maui. The people of the Ka'anapali district were "raising Hell" with the sailors from the Lahaina roadstead, drinking, carousing, neglecting the King's work. Ka-hekili mounted the cliff, a sacred burial cliff, drawing attention of all the people to himself and his death-defying intention of leaping off. The people believed in his divine origin and this was a dramatic show of his god-like character. The cliff itself was known as *'uhane lele,* "the leaping off place of the soul" or "the soul leaping" (to heaven). Ka-hekili survived the famous leap and, at least for a time, restored his people to their sober tasks. This story is one that was frequently told to Mrs. Inez Ashdown by descendants of Ka-hekili and others. Every evening at sundown, the Sheraton-Maui reproduces Ka-hekili's act in a ceremony of lighting the torches, blowing the conch shell and culminating in a spectacular leap by a hotel employee off the Keka'a cliff.

I found a good summary of the French landing on Maui in a small book published in 1959 by the Maui Historical Society, Wailuku. It is called *La Pérouse on Maui,* by Mathurin Dondo. In studying the journals, I came across the fact that the French ships

Boussole and *Astrolabe* were tacking on the southeast side of Maui, anchoring, and making their landing at La Pérouse Bay at the very same moment that Portlock and Dixon of the British Expedition were tacking off the Maui coast, and that from May 29 to June 1st, 1786, the four large European naval vessels could almost literally have bumped into each other; yet were not seen by one another. I have found no other source for this observation.

The journal of Nathaniel Portlock and that of George Dixon are especially interesting for their descriptions of meetings with King Ka-hekili at the time he resided on and ruled Oʻahu. Dixon spelled the King's name "Tereteere."

In addition to the journals of the European explorers, I read Kuykendall, Kamakau, and Fornander, along with more recent histories of Pacific exploration; i.e., Ernest Dodge's *Beyond the Capes,* Daws' *Shoal of Time,* and John Dunmore, *French Explorers in the Pacific,* Volume I, Clarendon Press, Oxford, 1965.

For Maui's history, Vancouver has provided in his journal the most detailed information on persons and events during those crucial years when Hawaiʻi's interminable wars were finally coming to a close. His journal, and those of his officers aboard H.M.S. *Discovery* and *Chatham,* are not only the most important historical sources available for those years, but are especially interesting because they provide a gratifying and positive chapter in the early relations between Hawaiʻi and the westerners who were by then coming to Hawaiʻi's shores in significant numbers.

CHAPTER 6

In addition to the general histories, I used many other sources, mostly missionary narratives or journals. Among these are Charles Stewart, Hiram Bingham, and William Richards, whose works are listed in the bibliography. An interesting account of Ka-ʻahu-manu's life is Kathleen Mellen's *Magnificent Matriarch,* Hastings, 1952. There are numerous though brief descriptions of the favorite wife in the journals of ships' captains who met her either at Kona or Honolulu, One of the most interesting is the touching story Vancouver tells of how he brought the estranged pair–the king and Ka-'ahu-manu, back together by arranging a meeting in the cabin of his flagship.

All descriptions and contemporary portraits of this Queen show her as being a very large woman in the mold of a Polynesian-Hawaiian Queen. Young Ebenezer Townsend, Jr. described her in 1798 as "a large woman with a great deal of the cloth of the country around her, which she also soon got rid of ..." At that moment, she was a visitor on the sealing ship *Neptune*. (*Paradise of the Pacific*. November 1936, page 23.)

Alexander's description (*Brief History of the Hawaiian People*, American Book, 1899) of "The New Ka-'ahu-manu" is interesting. "Scarcely less remarkable was the change in the character of Ka-'ahu-manu the Regent. Superior in intellect and in decision of character to most of the chiefs, she was haughty, overbearing and cruel before her conversion. At first she treated the missionaries with disdain but her mind became interested first in the novel arts of reading and writing and then in the new doctrines which they taught, and finally her heart and conscience were completely won over.

"As she did nothing by halves, the change in her conduct and in her treatment of her people was so striking that they called her 'the new Ka-'ahu-manu.' From the beginning of the Year 1825 she devoted herself with her wonted energy to the improvement of her countrymen, made frequent tours among the islands to promote education and to urge the people to the practice of industry and virtue." (p. 190)

Stewart, Richards, and Bingham are also the chief sources on Ke-opu-o-lani. Also Ellis, the Englishman who administered the last rites when the Sacred Queen lay dying at Lahaina. These Yankee missionaries are our chief sources on the princess Nahi-'ena-'ena whose modern biographer is Marjorie Sinclair, *Nahi-'ena-'ena*, Univ. Press of Hawai'i, Honolulu, 1976.

In this chapter I have mentioned that Kamehameha the First as he was dying appealed to his personal god (of war), Ku-ka-ili-moku. Though the Queen ordered destruction of the heiaus and images, the particular feather god-image sacred to the King was preserved as were other feather images of the Hawaiian war god. The image in the Bishop Museum, once in the possession of the American Board for Foreign Missions in Boston, is believed to be the one to which the dying king turned for help. Other fine specimens were preserved and are found in the collection of the British Museum of Mankind and in the Peabody Museum of Salem.

The quotation regarding the relationship between Kamehameha III and his sister is from the *Journal* of Elisha Loomis, Hawai'i Mission Children's Society, pp. 15-16, quoted in Sinclair, M., *Hawaiian Journal of History*, Vol. 3, 1969.

Queen Ke-opu-o-lani is still mourned by royal descendants and her people. Each year special services are held to commemorate the sacred queen beside her tomb at Lahaina. *Maui News,* December 9, 1977, p. 2, "The Ali'i Gather."

Another source for this chapter was Missionary Letters, III, 877, Richards and Stewart, 1828, Hawai'i Mission Children's Society, also Bishop Museum, and as found in typescripts in the files of the Lahaina Restoration Foundation. One especially interesting letter is that of Rev. William Richards to Commander Wilkes of the U.S. Exploring Expedition.

Again, I have drawn on Kamakau's *Ruling Chiefs* for material in this chapter.

It seems remarkable in studying the lives of the two great queens from Maui to note their apparent harmonious and almost loving relationship. Two very very different Hawaiian Chiefesses, two very different women, married to the same man, in a juxtaposition of personalities. Perhaps the relationship sheds some light on the Hawaiian attitudes and culture, their ways of thinking and loving and of marriage and their raising of children.

Ke-opu-o-lani's father was Prince Kiwala'o who was slain by the hand of Ke-e-au-moku, the father of Ka-'ahu-manu. The young high chief, Kiwala'o, was the rightful heir to the kingdom of Hawai'i which Kamehameha seized. One would think that Ke-opu-o-lani would have resented Ka-'ahu-manu. Yet Ka-'ahu-manu and Ke-opu-o-lani lived in perfect harmony after the death of Kamehameha. There seems to have been no jealousy on the part of

Ke-opu-o-lani, the mother of the successor kings. Both of these kings, though of higher rank than Ka-'ahu-manu were each in turn dominated by Ka-'ahu-manu who shared their rule of the Hawaiian Kingdom.

CHAPTER 7

The material now available on both the missionaries and the whaling era at Lahaina is voluminous. For Chapter 7, which barely scrapes the surface of Lahaina's story, I relied mainly on Kuykendall's *Hawaiian Kingdom,* Volumes I, II, and III, and Gavan Daws' *Shoal of Time,* and on Mary Charlotte Alexander's *Doctor Baldwin of Lahaina. Grapes of Canaan, Hawai'i 1820,* by Albertine Loomis is one of the best general works on the missionaries. It is published by the Hawaiian Mission Children's Society, Honolulu, 1966, and is available everywhere in Hawai'i in paperback.

A convenient source is the typescripts found above the offices of the Lahaina Restoration Foundation. These are in boxes accessible to scholars, though uncataloged. They are excerpts from the missionary reports; i.e., the journals of Richards, Stewart and others; books as well as reports, letters and diaries. Most all of the source materials are found (some in originals) in the Library of the Hawaiian Mission Children's Society in Honolulu, probably the best source on missionary history to be found in Hawai'i. The Journal of Charles Stewart is important for the early period, 1823-1825.

The study of Lockwood and Rossie Frost, *Rendezvous in Lahaina,* was a valuable source.

Although I have used the story of Kamehameha's paternity by Ka-hekili in this chapter, it is not an established historical fact. His mother, the young wife of Keoua, the brother of the King of Hawai'i, visited the court of King Kamehameha-nui on Maui where she met the King's younger brother and heir, Ka-hekili.

The story goes that, when she returned to the Hawai'i court, she was pregnant by Ka-hekili and the child, Kamehameha, was thus his son.

John Papa Ii was in a better position than other historians to know such things as he was a member of the inner court of

Liholiho. It was his opinion that Keoua was the true father. (Ii, John Papa, *Fragments of Hawaiian History,* Bishop Museum Press, Honolulu, 1973.)

The question can excite some strong opinions. On the Island of Hawai'i there are few who question that Keoua Kuahu-'ula, commonly called Keoua, was the great chief's father. But on Maui, Ka-hekili is more often named as the father. It might have suited the conqueror to lean to one or other view depending on the political circumstances.

Although there may have been political reasons either on the part of Hawai'i Island chiefs or that of the Maui chiefs with their strong ties to Kamehameha's high-ranking and favorite wives, the question is not unique in Hawai'i. There is an ancient saying that the mother's blood line is certain. The term *po'o lua,* divided or two-headed, was applied to the frequent cases where the father of a child could have been either of two men. Perhaps then, it was a case of *po'o lua* and "only the stars know" who Kamehameha's real father was.

I used material from the booklet put out by the Maui Historical Society, "The Story of Lahaina," and also referred often to the more recent booklet, "Story of Lahaina," an excerpt from a report prepared for the County of Maui by Community Planning, Inc. Inez Ashdown's "Stories of Old Lahaina" was helpful but more so were my frequent interviews and "talk story" sessions with Mrs. Ashdown who probably carries enough Maui history in her head to fill a shelf of volumes.

As for all my early chapters, S.M. Kamakau's *Ruling Chiefs* was handy and in some instances indispensable. But without Elspeth Sterling's admirable Index to Kamakau, I would have been lost more often than not. The Index, in paperback, is available at Book Cache, Kahului, and at the Vestibule Shop, Bishop Museum, Honolulu.

Some other books which I referred to for Chapter 7 are: Ernest Dodge's *Beyond the Capes* (Little, Brown, Boston, 1971), *New England and the South Seas* by the same author who gives a good short account of the American whaling in the Pacific in Chapter II, "Hunting the Cachalot." I consulted many others, among them the following: *The Whale* (Crescent, N.Y., 1974), *Journal of William Ellis* (Advertiser Publishing, Honolulu, 1963), F. Olmsted's *Incidents of a Whaling Voyage* (Reprint by Tuttle, Rutland, Vermont, 1969), Bradford Smith, *Yankees in Paradise* (Lippincott, N.Y., 1956), A. Campbell, *A Voyage Round the World, 1806-1812* (U.H. Press, Honolulu, 1967).

An interesting observer in the early nineteenth century was Jacques Arago, draftsman to the expedition of Captain Freycinet during the years 1817-18-19, and 20. His narrative was published in London in 1823 and his drawings of Hawaiian people and places are well known. Arago visited "Mowhee." He found Taourae (Kaho'olawe) "without the slightest vestige of vegetation,...deserted and uninhabited," but Lahaina he described as "like a garden." The Chiefess whom he met there received him with her daughter seated by her side "unencumbered with drapery." She "tempts you by her unsophisticated caresses." (p. 120). He wrote in a footnote: "we found all that can delight the species at Mowhee; while we met with all that amuses and attaches them at Woahoo...at Mowhee, the natives prefer a tranquil life, here (O'ahu) they are fond of agitation." (p. 122).

CHAPTER 8

My basic source for the early history of sugar in Hawai'i is Kuykendall, Volume I, *The Hawaiian Kingdom.* I also have quoted Daws' history here and there. Much of the material on the sugar industry on Maui is taken from the Centennial report of Wailuku Sugar Company 1862-1962, "A Century of Progress in Sugar Cane Cultivation." The sketch on Edward Bailey is from the *Missionary Album,* Sesquicentennial Edition 1820-1970, Hawaiian Mission Children's Society, Honolulu, 1969, pp. 34-35.

The section on Claus Spreckels on Maui came mainly from Kuykendall, Vol. III and Jacob Adler, *Claus Spreckels, The Sugar King of Hawaii,* UH Press, Honolulu, 1966.

For the stories of the Baldwins, I have also used Kuykendall plus *the Memoir of H. P. Baldwin* by his son, Arthur, privately printed in Cleveland in 1915.

I used the Alexander & Baldwin report "Seventy Five Years a Corporation, 1900-1975" and their publication "Ampersand" for Fall 1977 for information on their history and sugar production. I talked with officials of all three sugar companies on Maui and secured up-to-date information from them. The A & B monthly publication "Maui Today" was a source. Some of the material was taken from the Maui *News* and the Maui *Sun.*

On pineapple, I used local sources: the magazine Hawai'i Business' for August 1969 "Colin Cameron Takes Over at Maui Pine," the Annual Report of Maui Land and Pineapple Company for 1976, and discussion with Joe Hartley, President of Maui Pineapple Company.

I consulted many other sources for this chapter, among them, Ethel Damon's *Father Bond of Kohala,* Honolulu, 1927; *The Hawaiian Journal of History,* Volume 5, 1971 "King Cotton, the Spinning Wheel and Loom in the Sandwich Islands," and for the early Chinese sugar masters, Lin Yuke Char, *The Sandalwood Mountains, Readings and Stories of the Early Chinese in Hawaii,* University Press of Hawai'i, Honolulu, 1975, and Wai-Jane Char, "Chinese Merchant Adventurers and Sugar Masters in Hawaii: 1802-1852," *The Hawaiian Journal of History,* Vol. 8, 1974.

CHAPTER 9

The first part of this chapter is based on talks with Charles Pili Keau during several historical field trips, a taped interview, and an essay by Roberta Mercado, one of my students in a course in Maui history in 1976-77.

For the Chinese in Hawai'i there are excellent sources. These include the works cited for Chapter 8 and the small book, *The Chinese in Kula* by Diane Mei Lin Mark published by the Hawai'i Chinese History Center in Honolulu in 1975. This was my main source on the Chinese on Maui and especially the section on Sun Yat-sen. The material on "Uncle" Shinn as well as the stories of Alfred Boteilho and A.B. Sevilla are quoted by permission from the Mayor's report of 1976 and the men concerned.

References for the sections on the Japanese, Portuguese and Filipinos are *A History of the Japanese in Hawaii,* United Japanese Society, Honolulu, 1971; *Portuguese in Hawaii,* Multicultural Center, Honolulu, 1973; Bruno Lasker, *Filipino Immigration,* N.Y., 1969; *Immigrants in Hawai'i* 1976 State Immigrant Services Center, Honolulu, 1975; and, Sister Mary Dorita, *Filipino Immigration to Hawaii,* U.H. Thesis, 1954.

My principal guide for this chapter was A.W. Lind, *Hawaii's People,* U.H. Press, Honolulu, 1967.

Gavan Daw's *Shoal of Time* was the general source for the section on the haoles; especially the story of James Makee of Rose Ranch. Kuykendall, Volume IV, provided basic information.

Additional references on Sun Yat-sen in Hawai'i are Restarick, H.B., *Sun Yat-sen: Liberation of China,* Yale Press, 1931 and Lee, Shao Chang, "The Chinese 'suns' in Hawaii," *Paradise of the Pacific,* Honolulu, November 1937.

CHAPTERS 10 AND 11

Armine von Tempski's *Born in Paradise,* (Duell, Sloan and Pearee, New York, 1940) gives a fascinating picture of growing up on the big Haleakaia Ranch on Maui in the 1930's. Nearly all the characters in the book are dead except "Jackie," who is Mrs. Inez Ashdown.

A number of local people gave information on the period after World War I and during World War 1I. The story of the sinking of the military transport off Hana and the story of the air crash which resulted in the deaths of at least 20 marines on the ground are from Robert Schmitt's article "Catastrophic Mortality in Hawaii," in the *Hawaiian Journal of History,* vol. 3, 1969.

Nearly all the material on the Fourth Marines and Camp Maui was taken from *The Fourth Marine Division During World War II,* Carl W. Proehl, editor, Infantry Journal Press, Washington, 1946. This Press is no longer in existence but has been taken over by the Association of the U.S. Army in Washington.

The book is unusually well written and is profusely illustrated including many pictures of Camp Maui. It is out of print but available at the Kahului public library. I also interviewed two men who were stationed here with the Fourth in 1944-45.

My information on the men from Maui who served in World War II is from John A. Rademaker, *These Are Americans, The Japanese Americans in Hawai'i in World War II,* Pacific Books, Palo Alto, 1951, and Thomas D. Murphy, *Ambassador in Arms,* the *Story of Hawaii's 100th Battalion,* University of Hawai'i Press, Honolulu, 1954.

A more up-to-date reference is William Petersen's *Japanese Americans,* Random House, New York, 1971, from which I took the brief summary on the 442nd Combat Team. Strangely enough, I could not find out the statistics regarding armed forces service by men and women from Maui. *I mainly* wanted to know how many served altogether in World War II, how many served overseas from Maui, how many were lost (I finally got this figure by simply counting the names on the list posted at the Memorial Gymnasium), what honors or awards were won by Maui men for bravery, etc. I called and visited veterans of Foreign Wars, called the presidents of the 442nd and 100 clubs both on Maui and on O'ahu. They said there was no breakdown on the Maui figures. I called Veterans' Administration, Army Recruiting, County Information, and various individuals each of whom referred me to someone else.

The story about Eddie Tam is from the local newspaper accounts, mainly the *Advertiser,* Honolulu, December 14, 1966. *The Star Bulletin, The Advertiser,* the Maui *News,* were sources for information on Mayor Elmer Cravalho together with a tape of an interview he gave to me and my students in March 1977 and articles in *Honolulu Magazine* (April 1978) and *Hawai'i Business* (magazine), January 1978.

Quotes about the role of the County on Maui are taken from the Mayor's Annual Report for 1977. Material for Chapter 11 comes from current journals, newspapers, and the observations and opinions of the author during a decade of residence on the island.

Chapter Notes by Jill Engledow

In updating *Mowee* to include the years since its original publication in 1978, I relied primarily on research in the microfilmed copies of *The Maui News* available at the Maui Community College library. Based on an extensive reading of this microfilm collection, I wrote a series of articles on the newspaper's first century of publication which were published in the paper during its centennial year, 2000. I then used the compiled articles to bring *Mowee* up to date early in 2001.

In addition to knowing about events that happened after the publication of *Mowee*, I had the benefit of hindsight in reviewing some of the work Cummins Speakman had done about the years just before the publication. I deleted some of the items that now seemed less relevant and filled in areas that had, over the years, become more significant. For example, Chapter 8 includes new information about the development of Kahului. Chapter 11 includes revised accounts of the "hippie" era, the emergence of Kihei as a center of population growth, and the development of Ka'anapali, Lahaina, Kapalua, Wailea and Makena.

Revisions to the stories of Maui's major businesses were based in part on information supplied by the companies involved. For Alexander & Baldwin, Inc. and Maui Land & Pineapple Co. (Chapter 8), I consulted annual reports. For the resorts (Chapter 11), I used information supplied by their public relations departments.

I replaced one of the profiles Speakman had written with a profile of Toshio Ansai, based mostly on research in *The Maui News*. For the information on Ansai's family history I am indebted to his daughter, Carol Ball.

INDEX

Pu'u-kohola Temple, 44-45
Pu'u Kukui, 147
Pu-unene, 12; mill, 99, 105, 121

Q

Queen Charlotte, 48, 54
Queen Emma, 39, 99

R

Rademaker, John A., 183
Ranching, 86, 110-115, 127-128, 130, 141, 146, 148, 150, 183
Reciprocity Treaty, 96, 108
Reichel, Keali'i, 153
Religious freedom, 88
Rendezvous in Lahaina (Frost), 161, 163, 179
Republican Party, 118, 127, 128, 138, 139, 141, 142
Resolution, 1, 16-18, 20-26, 29, 31-33, 56, 90, 158, 161, 169
Reynolds, Stephen, 94
Rice, 93, 106, 120
Rice, Harold W., xi, 139
Richards, Rev. William, 70-72, 79, 83, 85-86, 176-179
Richards-Ha'alilio Mission, 85
Rikeke. See Richards, William
Riots, 79-80, 85
Ritte, Walter, 152
Ritz-Carleton, Kapalua, 147
Rollin, Doctor, 164, 170
Rose Ranch, vii, 127, 182
Rudkin, Charles N., 171
Ruling Chiefs of Hawai'i (Kamakau), 14, 40, 41, 62, 63, 76, 85, 164, 166, 167, 170, 171, 175, 176, 178, 180

S

St. Anthony's Church, 88. 122
St. Anthony's School, 111

St. Joseph's Church, 115
Samoa, 5, 52, 129
Samwell, David, 21, 164, 168
Sandwich Island Mirror, 92
Sandwich Islands. See Hawaiian Islands
Santa Cruz Islands, 53
Schmidt, Harry, 134
Schmitt, Robert, 182
Schools, 65, 69, 71, 72, 74, 83-87, 93, 95, 102, 103, 110-112, 116, 117-118, 121, 130, 140, 146, 152
Schussler, Hermann, 97-98
Science City, 152
Seamen's Hospital, 160
Seibu Hawaii, Inc., 148-150
Sevilla, A. B., vii, 120-121, 181
Shenandoah, 89
Sheraton-Maui Hotel, 174
Sherrod, Robert, 132
Shin, Shing Sam, 110
Shinn, Ten Sung ("Uncle Shinn"), 110-111, 183
Shoal of Time (Daws), 15, 35, 162, 175, 178, 182

Silk worms, 93, 106
Simpson, George, 170
Sinclair, Marjorie, 164, 176
Sinoto, Yoshiko, 124
Smallpox epidemic, 86
Smith, William O., 126
Society Islands, 5-6, 16
South Point, 5-6
Spanish explorations, 15-16, 21, 50, 87, 124, 166-168, 170, 173
Spanish speaking immigrants, 128
Spreckels, Claus, 96-100, 126, 180
Spreckels, Gus and Rudolph, 100
Spreckels, J. D., 99
Spreckelsville, 96, 99

ABOUT THE AUTHORS

Cummins Elliot Speakman, Jr. was born in Delaware in 1912, and from 1967 made his home on Maui close by the beach where King Ka-hekili welcomed the tall ships of Captain Cook more than two hundred years ago. His career included public relations, service in World War II, university studies, and teaching and academic administration in the United States and abroad.

Dr. Speakman came to Maui as President of Maunaolu College of Maui (1967–1971) and authored a history of international exchange in education.

Jill Engledow has lived on Maui since 1968. She worked as a reporter and copy editor for *The Maui News* for 17 years, and now operates Wordwright Writing and Editing Services. She has won several awards for her writing, including the Maui Historical Society's 2000 Preservatioon Award and a Certificate of Commendation from the American Association for State and Local History for a yearlong series of articles published to mark the 100th anniversary of *The Maui News*.